Classic Restaurants
OF
EVANSVILLE

Classic Restaurants

OF

EVANSVILLE

• • • • • • • • • • • • KRISTALYN SHEFVELAND

AMERICAN PALATE

Published by American Palate
A Division of The History Press
Charleston, SC
www.historypress.com

First published 2020

Manufactured in the United States

ISBN 9781467140850

Library of Congress Control Number: 2020930485

Notice: The information in this book is true and complete to the best of our knowledge. It is offered without guarantee on the part of the author or The History Press. The author and The History Press disclaim all liability in connection with the use of this book.

Contents

3. DINERS, DRIVE-INS AND COFFEEHOUSES

4. INTERNATIONAL AND TRADITIONAL CUISINES

CONTENTS

Preface

How does a non-Evansville native come to write a history of Evansville restaurants, past and present? When I was a graduate student at the University of Mississippi, my parents would travel south from their home in a westside Cleveland suburb, stopping in Evansville as the halfway point to enjoy a meal downtown and to view the barges on the Ohio River. Many times, my Dad joked that Evansville had two colleges, and when I graduated, wouldn't it be great if I ended up there? As luck would have it, when I graduated in 2010, a position at the University of Southern Indiana opened and it happened to be in my areas of specialty. In the intervening years since then, I have had the joy of getting to know this community and met many fantastic folks who have shared their family stories, their love of the region and their passion for making Evansville a great community now and in the future. Encountering many personal histories and great stories, I often thought to myself, somebody should be saving these, and thus I created *River Cities Oral History Project* to collect those traditions and memories for future generations. Some of the people that I've had the joy to get to know include Heather and Clint Vaught, entrepreneurs and visionaries for the renaissance of downtown Evansville, who shared, "We've been living and working in downtown Evansville since 2009, long before the redevelopment began. I've had a love affair with downtown since I was in middle school; frequenting a coffee shop where I first learned how to pull a shot of espresso in the building next to our current location! When we got married and were offered the opportunity to live in the building next door, we jumped on it! We had dreamed of having a coffee shop down in the lower level of our building since 2009 but were twenty-one and it wasn't a realization endeavor. Fast-forward to 2016, and we found ourselves back in the building once again where I was opening a handmade, local gift shop. We decided that since downtown was void of coffee at the time that this was our chance! It was a normal integration, as we had groups of artisans and makers already meeting and creating in our shop to enhance our shop with more reasons for people to meet, create, sip and shop." In *Classic Restaurants of Evansville*, I hope to share some of the histories of these wonderful places and to further the conversation about the wonderful stories in the Tristate.

Acknowledgements

R esearch assistance on this project came from the University of Southern Indiana Rice Library Archives and Special Collections, Evansville Vanderburgh Public Library, the Vanderburgh County Historical Society and the Willard Library Archives and Special Collections. Jennifer Greene, archivist at the University of Southern Indiana, played a special role in collecting images for this project. Existing materials from *Evansville Living* and the *Courier & Press* databases have been instrumental in documenting the history of the restaurants in the region, and through the generosity of community members, oral histories conducted with the help of University of Southern Indiana history students as part of the *River Cities Oral History Project* brought to light many details of the rich stories of classic Evansville restaurants.

Introduction

Are you in a pickle, with so much on your plate, that you just can't figure where to have your next dinner or lunch date? *Classic Restaurants of Evansville* can help. Nestled in a horseshoe bend along the Ohio River, Evansville finds itself in the border territory of the Midsouth and Midwest. This book considers the rich culinary traditions and foodways of the settlers of Evansville, Indiana, through the last two centuries. Evansville was founded in 1812 by Hugh McGary, who named the settlement after Colonel Robert M. Evans. Due to its location on the Ohio River and its abundant natural resources, Evansville has flourished over the last two centuries as the commercial, industrial, medical and financial hub of the Tristate region in this corner of southwest Indiana. By examining restaurants past and present—in images, recipes, food traditions and documentary evidence—this book highlights the rich history of Evansville's food traditions and diverse culture—from brain sandwiches to German traditions, cracker-crisp thin-crust pizza, Ski slushies, burgoo, doughnuts and more. In recent years, the area has experienced a revitalization movement in its historic districts through cafés, coffeehouses, and breweries—all hearkening back to Evansville's past while embracing the foodie movements of the present and innovating for the future.

It's said we are what we eat, but folklorists believe that what we eat symbolizes who we are. Food is central to our identities, and its customs, beliefs, production, preparation techniques and materials, display objects, rituals and traditions are cultural artifacts called foodways. Restaurant history and foodways can teach larger lessons about culture—geography, history, herbal lore and folk medicine, natural resources, the built environment, economics, tourism, climatology, religion, adapting and adopting in a multicultural society, environmental sustainability—and about tradition and change. Together, these topics can demonstrate how the family story, the community history and the significant events of humanity are regularly expressed through food, discovering the world through the types of regional food and the ways in which we connect to our past through them by the types of local restaurants that flourish in a region.

At its heart, this book is a story about Evansville and the places that evoke fond and colorful memories among its longtime residents, like Tom Kissel, whose father used to run a grocery store near the corner of Washington and Kentucky Avenues across from the famed Evans Cafe. In his recollection, "I remember many of our fine, and not-so-fine Evansville restaurants growing up, and hearing about others that I never experienced." His father bought Emge Grocery and ran it until 1971, when they moved the store three blocks away to Adams and Evans. Kissel fondly recalled, "I was eleven and clearly remember moving a grocery store, can-by-can." Many of the little confectioneries and hamburger stands are no longer in business, but a few remain, like the Burger Bank on South Weinbach and Covert, proving that a flat top and a fryer can go a long way and last several generations. And one simply should not forget the taverns. According to many residents of the Tristate, Evansville has the highest per capita number of taverns and churches to residents than any other region. While no scientific statistical study is available to date, anecdotally, the theory rings true. Each neighborhood has at least a tavern or two still in business and many, many more that have closed over the years. Those that remain have a long and storied history with family recipes and tall tales for generations to come. In fact, many of the bars in Evansville have multiple establishments within their walls, as in the 1980s and 1990s, several tavern owners made sure to save the physical attributes of closing establishments and bring them into the renovations of flourishing and expanding taverns and restaurants.

When considering expansions and renovations, one must touch on the events along Franklin Street on the near West Side. Since 2012, the Franklin Street Events Association has fostered the growth and reinvigoration of events and businesses on Evansville's West Side: "Our mission is to encourage, coordinate and enhance the development and promotion of quality art, small business growth and entertainment of every variety. We foster creative endeavors throughout the community and will position Franklin Street as a leading center for art, music, culture and entertainment." It has been a robust

Maiden's Brewery near Franklin Street, renamed Damsels in late 2019. *Author photo.*

success, as a number of new restaurants have opened and there are seasonal events alongside the most well-known local event, the West Side Nut Club Fall Festival, which raises money for charities each year through the sale of local favorites like pronto pups, chicken and dumplings and blackberry cobblers at individual charity booths. Colorful murals adorn several of the establishments near Franklin Street as well as downtown, a national trend of beautiful and eclectic images that are perfect photo opportunities for social media alongside images of dishes of food, perfectly plated. One such mural is on the side of Maiden's Brewery, now called Damsels, a recent inclusion to the Franklin Street region and a "full-service family friendly restaurant specializing in pub fare food and award-winning brewed on-premise beers. Proudly promoting Made in Evansville."

Nothing says Evansville quite like a jar of burgoo from one of the local BBQ joints, a slice of Ski pie from Marx's, fond memories of Sterling Beer in the taverns around town and cracker-crust pizza pies. Social media posts remember places like the Country School restaurants that served great breakfasts at two locations as well as stories about the Farmer's Daughter, an iconic lost legend alongside the famed F's Steakhouse and Café Venice. Café Venice opened in 1929 at 107 NW Third Street in Evansville and at one time specialized in steaks and chop suey. With an abundance of culinary traditions and restaurants, Evansville has a rich and varied history—this book only begins the discussion. Transplants from Kentucky brought with them barbecue traditions. One of these lost legends is Baugh's, which opened in

1934 under the direction of Floyd Baugh, who had arrived in Evansville that year from Kentucky. Baugh later sold the business to Bruce Hall and J.B. Render, who sold it two years later, in March 1946, to Kenneth A. McKinney, who renamed it Mac's Bar-B-Q, another lost legend much beloved by folks in the Tristate for the sweet barbecue sauce and pies, like chocolate, banana and coconut. McKinney sold it to his nephew William Skelton in 1972. After moving to 500 South Green River Road, Mac's closed down in 1993 or 1994.

When talking about foodways and restaurant histories with Evansville folks, memories include the trips with grandparents to Mac's Bar-B-Q, the Weinbach Cafeteria and Western Ribeye. Take, for example, an oral history conducted by the author with Kathy Oeth (Kuebler) an Evansville/Tristate native of at least three generations, who was born in Evansville, grew up in Mount Vernon and moved back to Evansville as an adult. Oeth recalled that every summer she went to the public swimming pool in Mount Vernon, which was built when she was in fourth grade, and then every Saturday going downtown with a girlfriend to buy a cherry phosphate and Grippo's BBQ potato chips at Culley's Pharmacy. Other memories included the North Main Drive In, a little ice cream stop where she loved to get chocolate hot fudge sundaes. Like many folks, Oeth went to Farmer's Daughter with her grandparents quite often, remembering that every waitress had a bow in her hair to match her checkered uniform, and Oeth chuckled as she remembered the bouffant-style

Baugh's Pit Bar-B-Q. *Courtesy of the Evansville Vanderburgh Public Library, James and Rosemary Geiss Collection.*

hair with those little checkered bows. Speaking of quintessentially Evansville/ Tristate items, she commented on hot German potato salad from the Gerst Haus, the soup and salad bar from Western Ribeye and the importance of neighborhoods, community and burgoo. Burgoo is a hearty stew made from beef, chicken, sometimes mutton, with seasonable vegetables. The best burgoo is cooked outside, typically made with vegetables provided by local farmers, like the fundraisers done at Mars Elementary School since the 1950s or out at St. Philip's. According to a 2016 feature *Evansville Living*, fundraisers that sell burgoo for fourteen to fifteen dollars a gallon make about 1,000 to 1,200 gallons of burgoo for their events each fall.

Cherry Phosphate Recipe

Wild Cherry Syrup
1 ounce (30 milliliters) glycerin
Water
1 ounce (30 milliliters) cherry bark
4 ounces (120 milliliters) cherry juice
10 ounces (300 milliliters) sugar

Mix the glycerin with 4 ounces of water; add to the bark and macerate for 24 hours. Filter the liquids off the bark and then add 4 ounces of warm water and macerate for another hour. Filter and add this extract to the first one. Add the cherry juice and, if needed, water to make 12 ounces of liquid. Dissolve the sugar in the liquid without any heat.

Wild Cherry Phosphate
1½ ounces wild cherry syrup
1 teaspoon acid phosphate
Soda water

In a 10-ounce glass, add the wild cherry syrup and the acid phosphate. Fill the glass with cold soda water and mix with a spoon if necessary.

Source: https://www.artofdrink.com/soda/cherry-phosphate

IN A CONVERSATION ABOUT CHANGES to the Evansville restaurant scene with Terry Hughes, president of the Vanderburgh County Historical Society, Hughes related that the Cross-Eyed Cricket on the W. Lloyd Expressway used to be the Muehlbauer Cafeteria run by Cletus and Catherine Muehlbauer for over thirty years. A popular burger joint called Hill's Snappy Service used to be at the foot of Main Street and Riverside Drive. Hughes continued,

> *The Lucky Dragon was a popular Chinese Restaurant for quite a while. The best barbeque sandwich in Evansville was Smokey Mountain on North Main. Burger Farm, Farmer's Daughter and Sir Beef were all part of Andy Guagenti's business. He also opened the GD Ritzy's in Evansville. During my college years, the Turoni's on Weinbach was the Forget Me Not (commonly called The Flower Shop)—a very popular college hangout. On Dogtown, I have a friend whose mother walked the bar at Dogtown when she was married (a West Side tradition). He also got his first sip of beer at Dogtown on his way home from being born (another West Side tradition).*

Neighborhood transformations like the reinvigoration of Franklin Street are a big part of the Evansville restaurant story, and another important place to consider is the historic cultural district known as Haynie's Corner, named after original resident George Haynie, who built a pharmacy there in 1888. Close to the Ohio River just east of downtown Evansville, the Arts District known as Haynie's Corner is actually four historic neighborhoods: Riverside, Culver, Goosetown and Blackford's Grove. As part of the revitalization of the community, Lamasco Bar & Grill owner (West Side staple on Franklin Street) Amy Word opened the Dapper Pig in 2015. Built in an 1885 Victorian home, the Dapper Pig was a farm-to-table restaurant that featured a menu built around seasonally available produce and meats that ensured their dishes were served at peak freshness and height of flavor. Inspired by Victorian traditions of excessive, eclectic and ornate decorations, the restaurant featured handmade chandeliers handcrafted from forks, knives and spoons as well as thousands of intricate and ostentatious pig figurines and ornaments tucked throughout the intimate dining spaces. The menu was true farm to table, focused on local vendors, which Amy Word told one interviewer amounted to about a quarter of the food budget, highlighting the importance of small farm–raised meats instead of factory farms. Amy Word recently sold Dapper Pig in 2019 to Sarah Wolfe and has since opened Amy's on Franklin, which features bespoke cocktails and decadent dishes in a fusion of midwestern and southern favorites. The site of the Dapper

Former Dapper Pig transforming into a new restaurant in Haynie's Corner. *Author photo.*

Pig became a new small-plates restaurant, Schymik's Kitchen, which opened in December 2019.

Kristen Tucker, founder of *Evansville Living* and the Tucker Publishing Group, was born in Iowa but moved to Evansville, her father's hometown, when she was seven. Her father's family was from Southern Illinois, but he grew up in Evansville on Florida Street and went to Central High School. A graduate of Castle High School in Evansville, Kristen grew up on the near East Side and has fond memories of monkeys in shoe stores both downtown and at Washington Square Mall. Speaking of foodways, Kristen related that it was a family tradition to pick up some fried chicken and go to the overlook in Newburgh near the lock and dam for a picnic. As a child, some of her favorite excursions were to go the Newburgh Country Store (most recently renovated into the Refinery Coffee Shop) and get the old-fashioned hard candies. Asked to describe a perfect Evansville day, Kristen related that she would prefer a nice spring day, as the trees have just a little of green but lots of pink and white buds. On that day, she might take the chance to sleep in a little bit, take her dog for a walk in the Evansville State Hospital Park, visit the Master Gardeners display garden, go to a Pilates class, then maybe go to a coffee shop like River City Coffee & Goods downtown and treat herself to one of the vegan pastries, afterward taking a stroll down to the greenway along the Ohio River to watch the barges. For lunch downtown, she could see herself eating outside at Bru Burger in the old Greyhound Station before allowing herself the treat of a drive in the afternoon, meandering through the countryside before settling back to her favorite pizza place, the Slice, over by University of Evansville. Her favorite? The spinach and feta. The perfect day might conclude with a concert or show downtown at the Victory Theater or at the Ford Center.

When considering Evansville restaurants and memories, the tavern culture is a frequent topic. On the surface, many of the taverns in town appear to have nearly identical menus—ice-cold beer, cracker-crust pizza, fried appetizers and hearty strombolis—but each has its own special spin on the favorites beloved by citizens who have long ties to the community and for their civic engagement in their neighborhood. Additionally, many of these establishments source their food locally from three major vendors that deserve to be a part of the story: Farm Boy, the Old-Fashioned Butcher Shoppe and Dewig Meats.

Farm Boy began as Mahon-Bonenberger Packing Company in 1952 and was co-founded by John Bonenberger. In 1966, his sons Robert and Richard took over and changed the name to Farm Boy Food Service. Farm Boy services Southern Indiana, Illinois, Kentucky and Tennessee and offers food products at wholesale pricing at its Food Mart at 2761 North Kentucky Avenue. The business is still locally managed by Robert and Richard, and they are training the third generation, Robert's son Mark.

The Old-Fashioned Butcher Shoppe is owned and operated by brothers Chris and Mike Baumgart, who are the second generation to run the establishment begun in 1983 by their father, Mike. All sides of beefs are from local farmers, sourced within a thirty-to-forty-five-mile radius. The brothers also have a full deli side to the operation, with hams, turkey and cheeses as well as sides like pimento cheese and potato salads.

Brothers Anton, Joe and John Dewig started Dewig Meats in 1916 in Haubstadt, Indiana, just north of Evansville. John's sons, Tom and Bill, took over operations in 1962. Bill retired in 1990, and Tom's family took over operations. Today, the shop is operated by the third generation of Dewig family meat processors. Their retail store boasts a literal smorgasbord of meats in a large market that has frozen, custom-cut orders, butchering and processing services as well as local wines, beer and snacks. In the freezer section, one can find Dewig's famous chili, which is also available at several local groceries, including Schnucks.

Before diving into some of the classic pizzerias, cafés and taverns in the Evansville metro, one must consider the history of Evansville neighborhoods, many of which were independent settlements before being absorbed into the City of Evansville. Neighborhood loyalty often determines how Evansville folks feel about different restaurants, pubs and, most importantly, pizza. At the heart of many Evansville neighborhoods and communities were their local taverns, pizzerias, and cafés. To give readers a sense of the region, one should also consider the various neighborhoods, and this map of Evansville neighborhoods highlights the various neighborhoods in the greater metropolitan area. Nowadays, Evansville folks are more familiar with the cultural districts—Downtown,

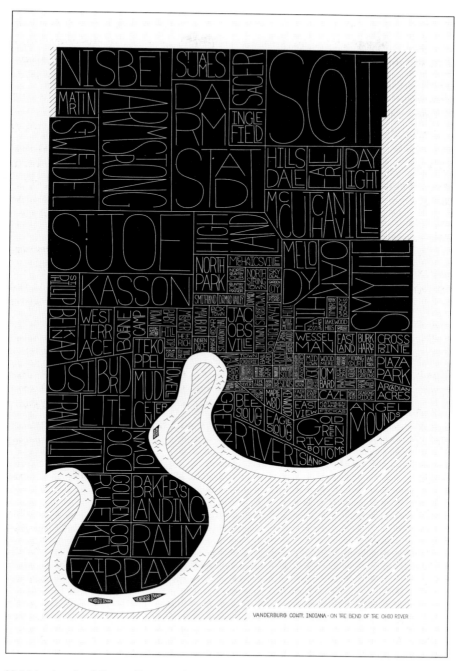

Neighborhoods of Evansville map. *Courtesy of Evansville Design Group, Rachel Wambach and Matt Wagner.*

Haynie's Corner Art District, North Main Street/Jacobsville, University of Evansville/Near East Side, West Franklin Street/Near West Side. The Evansville Vanderburgh County Community Map was commissioned by the City of Evansville's Department of Metropolitan Development and took over two years of research, including locating historic and new maps, utilizing Google Earth, Vanderburgh County GIS and United Neighborhoods of Evansville maps and visiting local neighborhood watering holes and interviewing citizens and public officials to find the true history and identity of many (sometimes obscure) areas of town. According to the creators, Rachel Wambach and Matt Wagner, "Each and every piece of land, region, district, or neighborhood has a unique and individual feel, based on many things from our past and our present. Our community is shaped and enlivened by the diversity of its contents; both people and places." Rachel and Matt have also been deeply involved in the Evansville Design Group, which is a not-for-profit organization formed to promote education, networking and enrichment within and among the local design community. Among their many missions to foster community engagement and memory, they design materials for the *Made in Evansville* campaign, the Owen Block Restoration Project, the West Side Nut Club Fall Festival, Willard Library and the Evansville Trails Coalition. The Made in Evansville Campaign has a shirt commemorating Funky's, a nightclub and restaurant that closed in 1980. When festival patrons see the Funky's shirt on the *Made in Evansville* table, a knowing look crosses their faces, a chuckle emerges and a blush creeps across their cheeks, before they furtively smile, steadfastly refusing to disclose what happened at the raucous disco in their youth.

1
Lost Legends

G one but not forgotten might be a better way to frame this chapter, as these much-beloved eateries have lasting reverberations throughout the collective conscious memory of the Evansville region. Through a combination of changing economic circumstances, social demographic shifts and different trends in eating habits, these popular spots all came to an end, but the memories remain.

THE BARGE

The Barge was a restaurant constructed out of an old river barge, rumored to be at least one hundred years old in the late 1970s. It was a popular spot for prom dates and ice-cold beers. Locals like to tell stories about the ice-cold tall boy beers available because the barge was technically on the Kentucky side of the Ohio River. Originally owned by Willard "Robby" and Wanda Robinson (who also owned and operated the Hilltop Tavern on the West Side), it was affectionately called "Robby's Barge" until September 1979. That year, new owners Dan and Martha Mawhorr moved the restaurant off the water to the Inland Marina. Floodwaters helped the process as the Ohio River surged over thirty-seven fee, and they sailed the six-hundred-ton barge onto a steel frame platform. Famed for catfish fiddlers, steaks and seafood, the restaurant unfortunately burned down in 1986.

Robby's Barge. *Courtesy of Evansville Vanderburgh Public Library, Evansville Courier & Press Photo Archive.*

DOGTOWN TAVERN

"Family style, you won't leave hungry!" beckoned a 1987 newspaper advert for this historic spot. Established in the late 1800s as a post office and a saloon, Dogtown Tavern—well south of the bend in the Ohio River—had a reputation for fiddlers from a Carr family recipe that lasted seven decades. The original owner was Joe Mesmer—an avid hunter whose pack of hunting dogs gave the location its nickname—but the building ended up in the hands of Joe Schenk in the 1880s. Schenk owned the spot until 1955, when Hillary Carr bought the tavern. His family operated the tavern until 2010. Susie Carr took over operations in 1981, then her son Mike Nunning took over running the restaurant in 2004. This Evansville landmark was south of the University of Southern Indiana along the Ohio River and directly across from downtown Henderson, Kentucky. Once known for hang-off-the-dinner-plate prime rib and German potato salad, this shuttered restaurant remains one of the most talked-about taverns in Evansville history. West Side novelist

Mike Whicker included the Dogtown in his 2001 World War II espionage tale *Invitation to Valhalla* as a spot visited by a Nazi spy.

In 1937, floodwaters were as high as ten feet into the restaurant. In a *Courier & Press* article from 1985, a favorite among locals, tavern regular Helen Buck stated, "We go all over looking for another Dogtown and we've never found it." Among the famed items on the menu were spoon bread, bread pudding, slaws and salads all made from scratch, but the most beloved were the catfish fiddlers and Katie's potatoes. According to the Carr family, Katie's potatoes was a meal of necessity during leaner times that became a beloved favorite.

Though Dogtown was open year-round, the busiest season was during the summer, when boaters would descend on the area. The prevailing theory as to why the Union Township location became known as Dogtown is that the porch used to be overflowing with hunting dogs. Many stories circulate around Evansville about the tavern, including a murder. In a 2008 *Evansville Courier & Press* article, local Reitz High School history teacher Jon Carl spoke of an 1896 incident:

> *Carl first heard of the incident when contacted by Bill Bartelt, now retired from Harrison High School. Bartelt sent Carl a newspaper clipping which described fisherman Zachary Willard as a "very mean man" with a bad reputation. On the day of the murder, he drove into town to sell his fish, then began drinking. Stopping on the road home, he heard of a political gathering near Dogtown. During the rally, he drank more, then got into an altercation with Henry Sanders, a young farmhand. They commenced to arguing,"* the newspaper story said, and *"applied mean epithets to each other." Willard pulled out a gun and shot Sanders "clear through the bowels." Willard took off in his boat, but was caught near Henderson.*

And the tavern was not just a favorite among locals—the owners like to hang pennants and maps with pins for all their out-of-town visitors from the states and around the world. In 1991, Michael and Jane Stern of the *Baltimore Sun* happened to be in the region and wrote affectionately about their experiences at the Dogtown, opining, "Dogtown is not a place most sightseers accidentally find themselves; but if you are moseying through the southern Midwest (indeed, a lovely place to mosey) and have a hankering for real American food, we suggest you seek it out." By all accounts, the old building and its cobwebs were charming in a greasy spoon, down-home cooking sort of way. The Sterns included a recipe for their favorite dish,

Katie's potatoes, which they described as "reminiscent of German potato salad," but their version is a full meal in a bowl, "top it with melted cheese, broken-up sizzled burger…whatever savory goodies you have on hand."

Potato in a Bowl (Makes 1 Serving)

Hot baked potato
1 tablespoon butter (or more, to taste)
Salt and pepper, to taste
1 tablespoon vinegar
1 tablespoon diced dill pickle

Optional
2 ounces cheese, melted
Crumbled bacon
Crumbled burger meat
1 sliced hot dog
½ cup cooked, chopped broccoli

Cut baked potato, including the skin, into bite-size pieces in a soup bowl. If it is mushy and doesn't cut neatly, don't worry. Toss potato (but don't mash) with butter, salt and pepper. Mix together vinegar and dill pickle. Toss with seasoned potato. Top with optional toppings of choice. Reheat if desired to melt cheese.

Source: https://www.baltimoresun.com/news/bs-xpm-1991-04-28-1991118099-story.html

EVANS CAFE

Famed for fried chicken for decades after it opened during the bustling World War II years, Evans Cafe was one of the city's most popular eateries, drawing customers from a fifty-mile radius. Located at 1010 South Kentucky Avenue along the busy Highway 41 (the direct north–south thoroughfare from Chicago to Florida), the restaurant was widely known for its home-style cooking, served at affordable prices in a clean, family-oriented environment. When Henry and Ann Evans opened the doors to the new business before dawn on October 23, 1943, the jukebox was blasting the song "Pistol Packin' Mama" as workers from the Evansville shipyard filed in to grab an early breakfast. Evans Cafe originally had only twenty-eight seats, but eventually seating capacity exceeded two hundred. In 1948, a Sunday dinner of fried chicken, two sides and a salad cost just seventy-five cents. The café also offered chicken and dumplings, roast pork and dressing and swiss steak sandwiches on special for eat in or carry out. In 1949, the spot advertised turkey and dressing

Evans Cafe. *Courtesy of the University of Southern Indiana.*

and invited diners to spend their Thanksgiving in the café. By 1960, the price had increased to ninety cents a meal, but the menu also expanded to fried chicken livers, fresh-baked pies and hot biscuits.

After 1984, the café closed and reopened several times under new owners. In the 1980s, the restaurant thrived as a community spot for senior citizens because of its familiar and consistently good food and its affordable prices. Favorite options included pork chops for breakfast as well as biscuits and gravy. In 1988, longtime manager Jean Tabor took over operations from Ann Evans. Tabor liked to keep the entire menu available any time of the day and brought a beloved vegetable soup recipe to the establishment as well as fresh yeast rolls. Ever popular in Evansville local's memory were the hearty chicken and dumplings.

Although it closed unexpectedly in 1990, another restaurateur, Fernando R. Tudela, the former manager of Weinbach Cafeteria, bought the site in 1991, and by 1992, the restaurant was back in business and back in a partnership with the Southwestern Indiana Regional Council on Aging to provide federally subsidized affordable meals to senior citizens. The senior meals program ran on Saturdays from 10:00 a.m. to noon. Many enjoyed the program, anywhere from 200–250 people a week, and some remarked

Changes to downtown Evansville, 1940s. *Courtesy of the Willard Library Archives.*

that it was like "coming home" for their meals. Patrons loved the community the café provided. While several individuals tried to make the restaurant thrive again, including an attempt in 2010 when Rosalee Barnes, under the moniker Cookie's Cookin, tried to revitalize the space with soul food and familiar fried recipes. Unfortunately, that endeavor failed, but a new Haitian-, Dominican- and African-inspired restaurant, Caribbean Cuisine, has opened in the location.

FARMER'S DAUGHTER

The 230 Main Street site has quite the illustrious and infamous history in downtown Evansville. Once part of the original public square platted first by founder Hugh McGary in 1814, the site held a jail, a courthouse, a school, a livestock pen and maybe even the gallows that saw the first execution in 1823—John Harvey, a murderer, whose bones are now at the Evansville Museum. Fire destroyed most of the buildings on the square in 1842, and in 1854, construction of the Washington Hotel began at 230 Main Street. By 1867, the hotel had closed, but a tobacco merchant, J.G. Sauer, took over the building for his tobacco and cigar shop. Expansions to the building included a sales room for crockery and Queensware that now houses Turley Jewelers. In 1870, another tobacco merchant took over, H.R. Schroeder, who used the fourth floor to manufacture cigars, and the Evansville Commercial College took over the second and third floors, remaining there for twenty-five years. The location changed hands again in 1877 when Samuel Vickery, a grocer, purchased the spot for a store that ran until 1886, when a clothing and tailoring business took over. During the early decades of the 1900s, it was a mixed-use space for more retailers, a dentist and multiple offices. Thom McAn's shoe store occupied the building during the 1940s and 1950s. In 1962, the Farmer's Daughter opened, beginning operations on the second floor.

The Farmer's Daughter, located at the corner of Third and Main Streets in downtown Evansville, was a breakfast and lunchtime staple for thirty years before closing in 1992. It was a second franchise for the established restaurant that succeeded on Highway 41 South. Both locations were known for their personalized attention to their customers and for being an affordable place to get a good meal. Favorites included filet mignon, steak sandwiches, ribeye and Big Lad sandwiches. For dessert, many Tristate residents fondly remember the cheesecake. The restaurants' slogan was, "Everybody loves the Daughter and we'd just love to have ya!" In the downtown location, baked goods were on display, with recipes from both the Farmer's Daughter and a local baker, Gus Parker, whose business was booming for twenty-eight years before coming on board at the Daughter in 1962. Committed to bringing the best of the best to customers, Daughter owner Andrew Guagenti teamed with Parker to go to the Durkee baking laboratory in Louisville, Kentucky, and the Swift Company baking laboratory in Chicago, Illinois, to test their recipes and make sure they were in top shape. Evansville diners reminisce about the many options downtown for a lunch treat, including the Farmer's

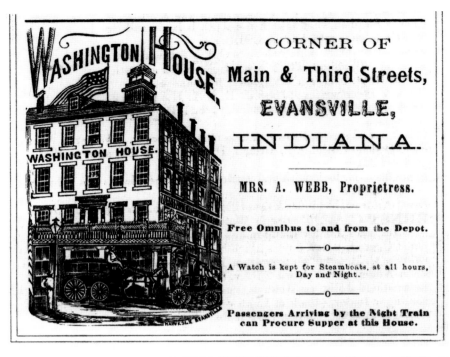

Above: Washington House advertisement (Farmer's Daughter). *Courtesy of the Willard Library Archives.*

Right: Farmer's Daughter, 1960. *Courtesy of the Willard Library Archives.*

Farmer's Daughter, 1984. *Courtesy of the Willard Library Archives.*

Daughter and Woolworth and S.S. Kresge on Main Street. Each had a countertop breakfast and lunch available. For many baby boomers, a trip downtown for school clothes and special occasions was not complete without a stop to the Farmer's Daughter.

The building was originally slated for demolition in the 1980s, but community organizers managed to save it. Efforts in the mid-2000s eventually led to the development of condominiums, and in 2015, a total overhaul of the site culminated in the opening of Comfort by the Cross-Eyed Cricket (see chapter 5).

F'S STEAKHOUSE

While Shing Lee was the first Chinese restaurant to open in town, Cantonese-style food in Evansville got its start at 125 Southeast Fourth Street, F's Steakhouse, which opened in 1948. F's started out as a café but evolved into one of the most popular steakhouses downtown until it closed in 1993. Spinach salads became a favorite menu item, but chief among local memory, however, are memories of the Chinese food. The story goes that

F's Steakhouse, Fourth Street view. *Courtesy of the University of Southern Indiana.*

F's Steakhouse. *Courtesy of the University of Southern Indiana.*

the owners brought the Cantonese dishes to the menu in the early 1950s, recruiting Cantonese cooks to Evansville to help master the dishes. In 1962, Li Wah Chong was the first recruit, and by the 1980s, several Chinese cooks had their start in the kitchen at F's, including John Koon Hep Chong and Lai Chong, who went on to open their own restaurant, House of Chong (closed in 2001, when she retired); Wen Yi Ma, whose family went on to start MA.T.888 China Bistro; Frankie Jung, who got his start at F's before opening Shing Lee downtown; and the owners of Canton Inn (See chapter 3). By 1987, twenty-five of Li Wah Chong's relatives had immigrated to the Tristate region, opening their own restaurants as far away as Mount Carmel, Illinois.

Cantonese was not the only menu option, however. Steaks, salads and made-from-scratch-daily soups were also popular. The *Courier & Press* published the following recipe in 1973, one of thirty-five soups day cook Mary Kirkman prepped for F's regularly:

Mulligatawny Soup

5 quarts water
2-pound fryer
½ cup diced celery
½ cup diced onions
¼ cup diced green peppers
4 chicken bouillon cubes
3 bay leaves
3 tart apples, cored and diced
2 turnips, peeled and diced
1 cup cooked rice
2 teaspoons curry powder
2 tablespoons chopped parsley
1 tablespoon cornstarch
Thick cream sauce
Salt and pepper to taste

Put 5 quarts water in soup kettle. Add whole fryer, celery, onions, peppers, bouillon, bay leaves, diced apples and turnips. Simmer until chicken is tender. Remove chicken from broth. Skin and dice fine. Return to broth and simmer until vegetables are tender. Add rice, curry powder and parsley. Thicken slightly with a tablespoon of cornstarch. Remove from heat and skim off excess fat. Add cream sauce and gently reheat, salt and pepper to taste.

Basic Thick Cream Sauce
1 tablespoon margarine
6 tablespoons flour
2 cups scalded milk
½ teaspoon salt
Dash white pepper

Melt margarine, add flour and blend until smooth. Add scalded milk, season and stir constantly until sauce boils. Cook about 3 minutes.

F's STEAK HOUSE OPERATED FROM this location for more than forty years until it closed in 1993. It was the first place in Evansville where you could order Chinese food, predating the first "official" Chinese restaurant by some twenty years. This building still exists, and a Korean and sushi restaurant named Jaya's Authentic Foods operates there today.

KENNEL CLUB

Evansville's Kennel Club at 5201 Kratzville Road in the North Side opened in 1926 and closed in 2019. The private dining room specialized in traditional favorites in an old-school establishment that paid homage to fine dining while occasionally dabbling in new traditions of global fusion–inspired dishes. What began as an association of individuals who shared a love of breeding, showing and hunting with dogs, the clubhouse was originally an old farmhouse on the hills and grounds where members would gather with their dogs to enjoy watching the hounds go through their hunting paces. Eventually, the Kennel Club opened membership to all Evansville residents, regardless of whether they owned hunting dogs. In recent years, the club menu was a composition of classics like steak, seafood and pastas with a regular infusion of specials placed on the members' calendars that leaned closer to the current trends by including newer dishes like Asian fusion plates. The highlight for many diners, however, was the commitment to old-school French techniques and dishes, including dishes prepared tableside in the classic manner, which was available to patrons from the public on Saturday evenings. In an October 2018 restaurant review in the *Courier & Press*, Michael Steckler, the bar manager and maître d', referenced his experience with tableside service at the Petroleum Club: "I went from server to catering director under Tommy Wilson, who was the maître d' at the Petroleum Club for 35 years. We did all kinds of things tableside, like Dover sole boned tableside, chateaubriand carved tableside, Bananas Foster, Cherries Jubilee." Like many Evansville restaurants, the focus was on local ingredients from surrounding farms and producers, such as sauces from Wilson's barbecue, produce from Joy Lane in Illinois and meats from Black Hawk Farms in Kentucky.

KIRBY'S OLD KENTUCKY BARBECUE

One of the first barbecue restaurants in Evansville was started by Kirby Williams of Hawesville, Kentucky, in 1920. In an oral history, descendants Mark Williams and Bob Williams told stories about their grandfather's establishment along South Kentucky Avenue. When Kirby passed away in 1937, his wife, Mabel, maintained the restaurant through World War II, until Alby Brougham bought the restaurant. Mark and Bob's uncle James "Jim" Louis Williams went on to start Kirby's Fine Dining restaurant in Haynie's Corner and, according to Jim's daughter Julie, always spoke fondly of how his father, Kirby, had a unique way of prepping barbecue using a self-fashioned smoker made from parts of cylindrical train car. Among his recollections, Bob Williams told stories about "dragging Main Street," which meant that he'd go out cruising in his car with a pretty girl for a bit before turning around and going back down Main Street to Riverside, continuing down to Kentucky Avenue, where you'd hit his grandpa's restaurant, the Humpty Dumpty, the Farmer's Daughter, Hamilton's Drive In and the first McDonald's restaurant in Evansville as well as the House of Como. Bob commented on what young couples could do in the 1950s and 1960s when sixty-five to seventy dollars a week was probably the average pay. He said there were three things you could do as a couple: have a nice car, have a nice house or go out to eat at fine places. Bob opined that you could not do all three, but if you were creative, you could work around your income and still have an active social life. For example, if you had the nice house and wanted to go out for a nice dinner, you could get reservations at the Elks Club, drive your old Model T car and walk two blocks to the Elks Club so no one knew you had an old car. In his recollections, Bob spoke fondly of F's Steakhouse and lunches at the YWCA. Bob also joked that Kirby's not only had barbecue mutton—hearkening to their Kentucky heritage—but also offered chicken. In later years, Bob said that it became a restaurant where you could buy drinks on Sunday, not legally, but he heard stories that it did. The restaurant scene on Kentucky Avenue used to be a popular destination for soldiers and paratroopers coming up from Kentucky. After the murder of Rudolph Ziemer, soldiers stopped coming up as frequently. Bob was a classmate of Jerry Turner's (Turoni's, see chapter 2) and is a 1960 graduate from North High School. Kirby's Old Kentucky Barbecue closed during the 1960s.

KNOTTY PINE

Dating back to 1894, the Knotty Pine Cafe was a community favorite in the North Main/Jacobsville neighborhood. Originally a confectioner's shop owned by J. August Ritter, by 1914, it was Becker's Confectionary, then Stewart's Confectionary by the mid-1940s. It became Todd's Cafe in the 1950s, a twenty-four-hour eatery with plate lunch specials run by Shirley Todd until it transformed once again to Dottie's in 1958 under the ownership of Harold and Dorothy Townsend. In 1962, it became known as Phil's Knotty Pine, owned and operated by Goebel Phillips; the spot was open until 2011. The site of the restaurant was demolished in 2015.

MATTINGLY'S 23

Hometown baseball hero Don Mattingly opened his restaurant, Mattingly's 23, in 1987 on Morgan Center Drive near the Showplace Cinemas in Evansville's East Side adjacent to the Washington Square Mall. Named after his Yankee jersey number, the spot featured sports memorabilia from baseball,

Right: Mattingly's 23 Don Mattingly Mural. *Courtesy of Evansville Vanderburgh Public Library, Evansville Courier & Press Photo Archive.*

Below: Mattingly's 23. *Courtesy of Evansville Vanderburgh Public Library, Evansville Courier & Press Photo Archive.*

basketball and boxing. The baseball legends area had tributes to Babe Ruth, Lou Gehrig, Joe DiMaggio, Thurman Munson and others. There also was a boxing ring with tables inside the ropes and a Hoosier Room, with tributes to local sports figures such as Don's late brother, Jerry Mattingly. The entrance featured a replica ticket booth, World Series programs and a souvenir stand. There was a gift shop that sold jackets, sweatshirts, T-shirts, caps, posters, coffee mugs, baseball bat pens, miniature bats, 1991 Coca-Cola Mattingly's 23 restaurant baseball card sets and more. The spot was popular during baseball season, but after nine years of operation, the restaurant closed in 1996. The menu featured pub and tavern fare from potato skins, steaks and fried combo baskets to the Build Your Own Yankee Burger and a New York prime rib sandwich.

PETROLEUM CLUB

In the 1930s, the Evansville region experienced an oil boom, and local oilmen would gather at the McCurdy Hotel at the end of a long day to socialize, culminating in the Evansville Petroleum Club Inc. forming in 1948. Club members eventually met in the Vendome Hotel, relocated to Citizens Bank Building in 1960, and in 1970, they found their final location in the Old National Building. Membership was not limited to oil and gas workers; by the 1960s, the membership included an even mix of many industries. The club was once the epicenter of business deals at lunch hour and the place to be when athletes, actors and other famous personalities came to town, including Tom Jones, Yogi Berra, and Roger Staubach. It was famed for servers who knew their clients by name and tableside Caesar salad preparation. Tommie Wilson was the maître d' at the club for thirty-six years and remembers the boom times, when men would come in and buy everyone's drinks. By the mid-2000s, however, club membership had dwindled, and the restaurant closed in 2006.

THE PUB

The Pub opened on March 15, 1978. For close to four decades, the Pub was a haven for families, Evansville politicians and businessmen, and according to legend, a few patrons even received their mail there. Longtime manager Larry "Bubbles" Pollock got his start managing the Rosedale Theatre at 1352 East Division Street when Larry Aiken purchased the adjacent Al's Bar in 1977. Aiken, and partner Tony Weller, who used to own a tavern called Hunter's Hideaway, worked to rehab the space by bringing in construction crews to take the building down to its studs and rebuild. A third partner, Bob Coleman, eventually came on board, and the Pub business boomed from day one as lunch, dinner and late-shift workers kept the place filled at all hours of the day. Popular menu items included pita pizzas and gyros. Many menu items were named for longtime patrons. Pollock took over management shortly after it opened and took over the business entirely by 1986, merging the establishment with the building that originally housed the theater. While the construction of the Lloyd Expressway split the Rosedale neighborhood in half in 1988, the Pub lived on despite smaller crowds, and Pollock kept the establishment booming with a banquet hall in the former theater space and a catering business.

At Pollock's 2015 retirement party, generations of Pub patrons shared their stories of Christmas traditions, wedding receptions, birthday parties, retirements, funeral wakes and divorce parties. For local Democrats, it was the unofficial meeting spot for politicians. While there were plans to continue the Pub under new management, the spot remains closed.

Pumpkin Delight Recipe

Crust
1 ½ cup graham cracker crumbs
⅓ cup sugar
½ cup butter

First Layer
¾ cup sugar
8 ounces Philadelphia cream cheese
½ cup milk

Second Layer
2 cups pumpkin
3 eggs, yolks and whites separated
1 cup sugar
½ cup milk
½ teaspoon salt
½ tablespoon cinnamon
1 envelope plain gelatin
¼ cup cold water

Mix the crust ingredients and spread in a 9x13 pan. Combine the ingredients for the first layer and pour over the crust. Bake for 20 minutes at 350 degrees. For the second layer, cook the pumpkin, egg yolks, ½ cup sugar, milk and spices until thickened.

Dissolve the gelatin in cold water. Beat three egg whites with remaining ½ cup sugar until they're fluffy. Add gelatin to pumpkin mixture. Add pumpkin to egg whites and fold. Spread on top of cream cheese mixture and refrigerate.

—*Evansville Living*

TENNESSEAN

When the Tennessean restaurant was sold to Dan Robertson in 1977, the *Courier & Press* asked original owner Grady Copeland why he and partner Eugene Gorman chose the name. Copeland mused that they received a telegram that read, "The Tennessean is the name to be, because both boys are from Tennessee." Copeland thought their wives sent it. Gorman and Copeland's restaurant experience began with Hill's Snappy Service in 1930, Evansville's first hamburger shop, selling nickel burgers. The Tennessean opened at 313 Locust Street in 1949 and became one of the most popular eateries in Downtown Evansville with its long counter and glazed tile wall. A second location later opened at 101 NW Fifth Street, which became the Flying Saucer in later years. The Flying Saucer, owned by Lana Utley in the late 1990s, hosted art exhibits, poetry readings and live music. University of Southern Indiana instructor of journalism Erin

The Tennessean.
Courtesy of the Willard Library Archives.

Gibson fondly recalled that her first date with her husband, John, was at the Flying Saucer, where she had blue corn chips for the first time. Later, her band, the Toddlers, would play there several times.

The Tennessean's patrons included businessmen, politicians, shoppers and students from nearby Central High School. In 1955, Copeland and Gorman built the second location at Fifth and Sycamore. On the menu were the ever-popular hamburgers, sometimes called splatburgers for the way in which they hit the grill and were smooshed by the spatula, with a copious order of greasy fries. Locals also remember the Polish sausage, chili and country-fried steak. Over the years, the Formica countertops became so well worn due to frequent customers and use that the shiny top faded to the duller black underside. But among many Evansville natives, that worn appearance was a part of the charm.

Socioeconomic changes to downtown affected the Tennessean. In 1983, John Baker took over the Tennessean at 313 Locust, and in 1987, he hoped to boost business by keeping the spot open twenty-four hours. Baker relished the greasy vibe of the Tennessean, remarking that the place was always a middle ground for folks from all walks of life to meet and hash out politics and business. Business and political wrangling took place there, especially in the back room. By 1995, however, the building was slated for demolition for a new parking garage. Despite community efforts to save the location, the site was razed in 1996. Parts of the Tennessean live on, however, as loyal customers and community members bought up parts of the interior and exterior, including the cooking equipment; the exterior neon sign, which sold for $1,000; ketchup and mustard dispensers; and dinnerware, which sold for $2 to $10 per piece.

WEINBACH CAFETERIA

Mel Singer's Weinbach Cafeteria opened in 1963 in the lower level of the pharmacy of the Weinbach shopping center. The restaurant was at the height of 1960s fashion with imported lighting from Italy and smoky brown tile floors with coral and walnut furniture. The food service area had tiled walls in aqua, beige and white. Three hundred people could be served in the dining room, while a separate banquet room could seat eighty. The Weinbach Center was the place to go for back to school shopping, and for many years the cafeteria played center stage in the memories of several generations of Evansville locals. In a circular ad from the *Evansville Courier & Press* in 1996, local female high school students were slated to model the latest fashions: "Think school, think Weinbachs." A popular lunch and dinner establishment, the cafeteria was also the go-to spot for many families after church. Menu items included a wide array of salads (kidney bean was a favorite), homemade pies, apple dumplings and custards. Visitors could choose between six and ten different meat options, including lasagna and chicken broccoli casserole, with dozens of vegetables, whose colors, one reporter opined, "present an array of color as pleasing as those of the room's furnishings." It also had an adjoining snack bar and soda fountain.

In 2004, former restaurant manager Fernando Tudela took over ownership; he also owned the Evans Cafe at one point and the Cross-Eyed Cricket, where they continued to use the yeast roll recipe from the Weinbach Cafeteria. Changing circumstances for the Weinbach Center forced the cafeteria to close in 2008.

2

Pizzerias and Taverns

averns and pubs played an integral part in American history, acting as
meeting halls and political spaces that played a pivotal role in American
politics and culture. As taverns were gathering places for communities,
scholars have argued that they upended elite culture by providing spaces
that intimately connected people of all ranks from the colonial period all the
way to the present. Neighborhood taverns and pubs used to adorn nearly
every street corner in Evansville, and the ones that remain are anchors
in the region. Included in this chapter are also discussions on Evansville
pizzerias, sometimes also taverns. Evansville has a unique, always delicious,
midwestern take on pizza, the Una style, which is a thin, cracker-like crust
with lots of cheese and heaps of toppings, cut into small squares.

DEERHEAD TAVERN

The Deerhead Tavern on 222 East Columbia Street has been a favorite
pizzeria in the Tristate since the early 1980s, when Dan Kollker expanded
a circa 1884 building that was originally the John Willem grocery store
into a sidewalk café, pizzeria and live music space. Kollker was among the
first to have a carry-out window in an establishment that sold liquor. The
Deerhead offered sidewalk seating and was the first to bring a Mardis Gras
celebration to Evansville, a tradition that Kollker continues at the Knob Hill

Tavern. Kollker has a long family history as a restaurateur. A 1966 graduate of Memorial High School, he earned a degree in 1970 from St. Edward's University in Austin, Texas, before coming back to Evansville to take on the restaurant business with his father, who owned the Town Pub, which used to be in downtown Evansville by the old courthouse and coliseum. Growing up, Kollker would spend his Sundays helping his dad clean up. When Kollker graduated from college, his father owned another restaurant called Steve's Inn on Green River and Washington. During the '70s, that intersection was one of the busiest places in all of Evansville, with the Washington Square Mall newly opened and Lawndale shopping center right across the street. Kollker worked there during high school and after college. Tavern food was on the menu, and Kollker brought some of those recipes with him to the Deerhead and then later to the Knob Hill Tavern. Kollker bought the Deerhead bar with his father and brother in 1982. At the time, the bar was in pretty rough shape and required extensive remodeling, and Dan took over the project by fixing up the existing building and bought up the lots beside it and across the street to expand and for parking. He went into partnership with Smithy McGinnis in 1984 to run the food end of the operation while Kollker ran the bar end of the tavern before Smithy went on to run other restaurants, including the Main Street Exit. Smithy's brother, Brad

Deerhead Tavern. *Author photo.*

McGinnis, was the carpenter and craftsman responsible for much of the renovation. During the renovation, they found a bar from the Kum Back Inn on Division Street, an old bar that was being torn for the Lloyd Expressway, and brought the bar to the Deerhead. They expanded the building to the deli and put up the canopy for the sidewalk café. This was before the State of Indiana allowed for outdoor seating, which became very popular with the lunch crowd from nearby Deaconess Hospital. Kollker's pizzas were inspired by the Una style of thin-crust pizza and quickly became a regional favorite. Evansville has a long history of being a test market for national franchises, and when McDonald's was testing a pizza option, analysts from *Pizza Today* magazine came to the Deerhead to sample the pizzas because locals told the visitors that Deerhead had the best pizza in town.

Since 2004, Chuck Johnson has owned the Deerhead, bringing with him a long history of pizza experience. Johnson started at Turoni's at the age of fifteen, spending thirteen years working at both the Main Street location and the Forget Me Not location on Weinbach Avenue before buying the Deerhead from Kollker. Since the Kollker era, the Deerhead menu has always had an eclectic flair, including Greek salads and a Greek souvlakia pita sandwich (marinated and grilled pork or chicken with tzatziki and veggies), while Johnson brought in cheese steaks and German bologna, as well as fried catfish and tenderloins. Among local favorites, however, are the pizzas. One of the most famous pizzas is the double-decker, which can be made with any choice of ingredients. Two thin-crust pizzas are assembled and then baked together after the center crust is parbaked. The Deerhead's specialty pies include the Jazzy Pepper Paradise, which hosts a smorgasbord of red and yellow bell peppers, banana peppers, pepperoncini, jalapeños, bacon and ham, all on the signature thin crust. Another favorite? The quintessentially Indiana pork tenderloin sandwich, much beloved by any true Hoosier.

DOC'S

Doc's (1305 Stringtown Road) started out as Domino's Tavern, then became the Alibi Lounge and is now under the ownership of Josh Pietrowski and his partner Cory Edwards. It seeks to be the go-to sports bar with an extensive menu of beer and wings—deep fried and sauced with homemade recipes. Pietrowski spent five years as a brewer at Turoni's, including two years as the master brewer. Pietrowski and Edwards also own the Evansville Brewhouse in Haynie's Corner. Doc's pork tenderloins, ground beef and wings are locally sourced from the nearby Old-Fashioned Butcher Shoppe. Also on the menu are pizzas and strombolis.

HAGEDORN'S

Hagedorn's Tavern at 2307 West Franklin Street was housed in one of the oldest buildings along the corridor. Due to structural complications, the original building was demolished, but there are plans for a new building that will retain the Hagedorn's name and continue the tradition of family-friendly tavern food and West Side favorites. The gable-fronted original building was built in 1883 for Phillip Mundo, who used the space for a wine and beer saloon below a boardinghouse and his personal residence for his family. It was a saloon until 1892, when Mundo began leasing out the premises to proprietors selling liquor and, during Prohibition, vendors who sold ice cream and soft drinks. It became Hagedorn's Tavern in 1925 and was a popular corner tavern among many in the West Side that catered to workers at the local sawmills, furniture factories, coal mines and textile mills. Plate lunch specials included pork roast and dressing, smoked ribs and krauts, and the Indiana classic, hand-breaded fried pork tenderloins.

HILLTOP INN

The Hilltop Inn is one of the most iconic Evansville restaurants. It has enjoyed a long and storied history from its perch on the top of the hill at 1100 Harmony Way on the West Side in Perry Township, historically known as Perryville and by 1874 commonly called Babytown. The moniker came from a story told by George Marx Jr. of a whiskey salesman who was looking for a room at the inn. George Marx Sr., then owner, regretfully told the salesman that no rooms were available, as they had just had their tenth child. Seeking accommodations elsewhere at the home of John Reiss, he found the Reiss family had just had their sixteenth child, with no rooms to let. According to a December 10, 1984 *Evansville Press* article, the salesman quipped, "I thought this was Perryville but it must be Babytown." Since 1839, this location has been a stagecoach stop, a saloon, a feed store and, for the last century, a

Hilltop Inn. *Courtesy of the Willard Library Archives.*

tavern and restaurant famed for its German heritage–inspired delicacies, including the famous fried brain sandwich, which was featured by Alton Brown on the Food Network and Asylum.com, which in 2009 gave the space the nickname "the manliest restaurant in America." There have been many owners: Jim and Barb Muensterman, Don Snyder and later his daughter Marta Hollen and, more recently, the Marx Barbecue family and friends have once again come to own the space. All of these owners have focused on retaining a familiar menu and family-friendly atmosphere that generations have come to cherish.

On the tavern side, the massive oak bar came into the space in 1939–40, salvaged from an early twentieth-century tavern on Pigeon Creek that was torn down by Evansville Lumber Company. The menu has included lunch and dinner specials of plates of ham, dumplings, catfish fiddlers and fried chicken, dressed with sides of heaping mashed potatoes, green bean, and fluffy dinner rolls. The salad bar is a particular favorite at lunch, as are tavern appetizers like fried onion rings, jalapeño poppers and breaded mushrooms. This new era will bring other favorites to the menu, including the Marx Barbecue pork grenades and its famous burgoo. What has kept the Hilltop popular is that the several owners have always added a few new items while maintaining the classics, keeping the famous tavern popular for generations to come.

HORNET'S NEST

The Hornet's Nest was a stagecoach station in the mid-nineteenth century, and local lore claims that the spot was named for an annual invasion of hornets in the settlement, then known as Earle. Once a rough-and-tumble settlement, the Hornet's Nest sits on the site of Lapsley's Saloon, the setting for a massive barfight on Christmas morning in 1877 between several Methodist patrons, including one Dr. Thomas Worrall, the resident physician, and James Grimwood. As the December 26, 1993 *Courier & Press* article by Ken McCutchan notes, "It seems that somebody said something uncomplimentary about somebody's sister." The original building burned down in 1926, but Oscar Sanders rebuilt on the site. Sanders's tavern, dining room and dance hall continues to be a favorite spot on Evansville's North Side. The menu has everything from comfort fare to fusion-inspired chef specials and an extensive beer list and delicious and decadent desserts. On the regular menu are the favorites of prime rib, golden fried chicken and Steaks à la Earle with sautéed onions, red and green peppers and mushrooms. Sandwiches include the hot brown and fried pork tenderloins. More recently,

Hornet's Nest.
Author photo.

the Hornet's Nest has become a destination spot for its brunch menu, which includes the Nest Benedict, a mortadella breakfast sandwich, chicken and waffles, an iced fishbowl Bloody Mary and the Wake Up In Earl coffee—mixed with brandy, Amaretto and Bailey's topped with cream. The Hornet's Nest operates under the phrase "Come for the history and delicious food, stay for the ambiance—you won't be disappointed."

HORNVILLE TAVERN

A North Side institution surrounded by farmland, with a spectacular view of sunsets, the Hornville Tavern on 2607 West Baseline Road has roots dating back to the 1930s. Nestled in a series of small buildings, the restaurant reminds patrons, "If we didn't cook it, don't eat it!" Currently owned by Butch and Deb Schneider, the menu boasts smoked chicken, ribs and thick-cut pork chops. The Schneiders bought the tavern in 2008 from Larry Luigs, who is credited with reopening the spot after a lengthy closure and ran it successfully for seventeen years. The Hornville has an extensive catering menu that accounts for about a third of the business. Among the tavern favorites on the regular menu are breaded mushrooms, ham and cheese hoagies and a barbecue chicken salad heaping with fresh vegetables and cheese. As with many Evansville taverns, the beer list is impressive and served in ice-cold fishbowls. Hornville Tavern is popular with locals and visitors—portions are big and generous!

Hornville Tavern.
Author photo.

KIPPLEE'S STADIUM INN

Known in the mid-twentieth century as Harold's Tavern, the moniker of 2350 East Division Street on Evansville's East Side changed to Harold's Stadium Inn with the 1956 opening of Roberts Stadium. A popular tavern owner, Harold Evans was a close friend of H.O. Roberts, mayor of Evansville from 1952 to 1955 and head of the Tavern Owners Association, which worked at the state level in Indianapolis to pass legislation favorable to the booming tavern businesses statewide, including laws that allowed women to sit at the bar and to serve as bartenders. In 1972, Larry Bitter purchased the establishment, renaming it Larry's Stadium Inn, and further capitalized on its proximity to Roberts Stadium by offering free bus rides to University of Evansville basketball games and late-night dining until midnight. Roberts Stadium was an iconic Evansville event space, hosting major rock concerts from the likes of Led Zeppelin, Bon Jovi and Elvis Presley. Lining the wooden booths are the carved initials of patrons from decades of popularity. In 1989, Bitter sold the place to Chip and Bart Schutz, who renamed the tavern Kipplee's Stadium Inn, remodeling the building to make the place more family friendly. Chip Schutz ran the establishment with his wife, Laurie, until Matt Klees and his wife, Kaycey, took over operations in July 2019. Matt Klees brings with him plenty of local restaurant experience, including several years at Turoni's on Main Street. Located throughout the restaurant are a number of images of the restaurant throughout the years as it grew into a popular spot along with Roberts Stadium and the UE Aces basketball team. Kipplee's is known for its thin-crust pizza, strombolis and salads. Although Roberts Stadium was demolished in 2013, Kipplee's is still a popular neighborhood establishment on Evansville's East Side and participates in student fundraisers for local schools and youth groups. According to a recent *Courier & Press* interview, "The main thing is consistency of product," said Matt Klees. "We are lucky to have kitchen managers who have been here a long time, and I'm not re-inventing the wheel. We're not touching the pizza, strombolis, ham and cheese or grilled chicken. Also, it's about treating customers like they are important. We're lucky we have so many options on where to eat in town, and if customers don't feel important to you, they'll just go somewhere else."

KNOB HILL TAVERN

Located just to the east of Evansville in Newburgh, Knob Hill Tavern has been beckoning patrons with its neon sign offering Hot Fiddlers since 1943. Current owner Dan Kollker is an Evansville restaurant pro, with previous experience at the Deerhead Tavern and his father's restaurants—he grew up in the business. He even brought one of his father's recipes to the menu: fried chicken livers in a mushroom wine sauce, one of Kollker's favorite dishes. Kollker bought the tavern in 1991 after an offer came up to purchase and reinvigorate the beloved establishment. Many other interested parties wanted to buy the place for its location and demolish the joint to build something new, but Kollker had other plans. He wanted to remodel but also preserve, to bring the Knob back to its heyday and keep as much of the original character to the building as possible. Kollker expanded, adding a new, larger kitchen and an outdoor dining area. The Knob is especially popular during Lent because of its varied menu offering the ever-popular catfish fiddlers with a heaping side of coleslaw as well as bourbon-glazed salmon and grilled mahi-mahi with mango salsa. Fried kraut balls come from a family recipe of cream cheese, kraut, onion and breading deep fried

Knob Hill Tavern. *Author photo.*

and served with a side of horseradish sauce. The Knob also has an extensive whiskey and beer selection, and Kollker brought his traditional Mardi Gras menu—and an Oktoberfest menu in the fall—from the Deerhead. The Knob Hill Tavern is located at 1016 State Route 662 W in Newburgh and is a customer favorite. When asked how he might spend a free day, Dan commented that even though his son has taken over the restaurant, Dan still comes in every day to check on operations, have a drink with friends and enjoy the space, just because he really likes coming over and feels very lucky to have had such a rich life with so many opportunities. In 2012, local actor and director Michael Rosenbaum, who portrays Lex Luthor in *Smallville*, chose the Knob to film his homage to his hometown, *Back in the Day*, about a Castle High School reunion.

LAMASCO

Lamasco's has been open since 1934 and is a favorite spot on Evansville's West Side (1334 West Franklin Street) for late-night pub grub and live bands. The owner, Amy Word, is the creator of the Franklin Street Event Association and the former owner of Dapper Pig. She has recently brought another venue to the West Side, Amy's on Franklin, a down-home comfort food venue for twenty-one and over patrons with midwestern favorites informed by Word's love for the cuisine of the Deep South, New Orleans, Texas and Mexico. Amy purchased Lamasco from her aunt and sought to develop the storied establishment into a music venue. Popular items include the breakfast menu, which includes omelets, burritos, chicken and waffles and biscuits and gravy. Philly steak subs, house-made chili, pork tenderloin and burgers are also popular along with pizzas and wings. The drink menu includes the Nutty Coconut, "Nutty just like your Lamasco crew."

Wednesday's at Lamasco have been a big hit for team trivia, as groups of all ages gather to answer a series of six rounds with three questions each about topics ranging from biology to popular culture while enjoying the hearty bar fare. From heaping plates of nachos to customized dishes of smothered chicken fingers covered in chili, queso, shredded cheddar cheese and copious amounts of jalapeños, the dishes are quickly polished off by patrons enjoying their time competing and hanging out with their buddies and the tavern crew. The staff members are congenial and know their regulars, stopping by the tables to double check to see if patrons want a round of their favorites or if

Lamasco Bar & Grill. *Author photo.*

they'd like to switch things up that night. Trivia participants are a jovial bunch, lobbing friendly insults across the room as the emcee plays music requests between rounds. Karaoke night immediately follows.

LEROY'S

At 2659 Mount Vernon Ave sits Leroy's Tavern, owned and operated by the Baize family since 1970, beginning with Leroy and Shirley Baize. Leroy Baize passed away in 2011, and the tavern is currently run by his daughter Terri Carl. Adorning the walls of the tavern are pennants, memorabilia from area high schools and local Indiana teams. Leroy's has your typical pub grub, including cheeseburgers, hot wings and pizza. On the menu are also egg rolls, bean soup and a patron favorite, the house-made chili from Shirley Baize's recipe. Its location near the University of Southern Indiana makes it a favorite with college students and professors, who can play pool or darts, watch sports, have access to free Wi-Fi and—on Fridays and Saturdays— warble out some karaoke. Leroy's is an active member of the Franklin Street Events Association, a group that has been focused on revitalizing community engagement on the West Side with family film nights, festivals and markets.

NISBET INN

Located on the North Side in Armstrong Township outside of Haubstadt, the Nisbet Inn opened in 1912 as a family business when George Maurer built the inn in 1912. Dutch and Mary Hollander ran the inn from 1939 to 1944, and the Straub family operated the business from 1944 to 1972. Jeff and John Salat bought the Nisbet in 1989, and its current owners are Becky and Jim Harl. The inn was named after a man called Nisbet who helped build the Evansville, Mount Carme and Northern Railway, and it has the second-oldest liquor licenses in the state of Indiana. Originally a multiuse building with a grocery store, a tavern in the center and a hardware store on the other side, the business is now a favorite sunset viewing spot with its wide porch, and the menu is famed for the coldest beer in the region. At a recent 100th anniversary party, Danielle Straub, who grew up in the restaurant, remembered prepping sandwiches for patrons. "We sold sandwiches in the tavern portion," Straub said. "We closed at six o'clock and we girls made the sandwiches, and we got a penny to keep for each one we sold. I remember the place so well….The old hand-crank phone was on that wall right over there."

Nisbet Inn. *Author photo.*

The Nisbet Inn has always been owned by people who were familiar with its history and wanted to keep the legacy going and maintain favorites on the menu. These favorites include a German bologna platter, a rib meat gumbo, sandwiches and plate dinners. In May 2011, an F2 tornado tore through Posey and Vanderburgh Counties and the Nisbet Inn had to undergo some serious repairs, including the entire second-floor front porch. Referencing the importance of the historic preservation in remodels, Becky Harl told *Evansville Living* in 2016, "We hope to be good caretakers of the building, and one day, turn it over to someone else who will do the same. Sometimes people come in and want to change everything and ruin the good stuff. We have not changed the ambiance. We have a responsibility to keep it as original as we can to still be functional."

Nisbet Inn Bean Soup

3 meaty ham hocks
3 bay leaves
2 teaspoons red pepper
Salt and pepper, to taste
Garlic salt for sprinkling ham hocks
1 large onion, chopped
½ stalk celery, chopped
½ cup celery salt
2 gallons canned great northern beans
½ gallon diced tomatoes

Boil ham hocks, bay leaves and red pepper 2 to 2½ hours in water to cover. Add salt and pepper to taste. Take meat from broth; sprinkle with garlic salt. Strain the broth; add onion, celery and celery salt. Boil 15 minutes.

Add beans and diced tomatoes. Simmer 30 minutes. Debone ham hocks; sprinkle meat again with garlic salt, then add to broth. Simmer 30 minutes more.

—*Evansville Courier & Press*, October 13, 2006

PEEPHOLE

The Peephole Bar & Grill open in September 1969 under the proprietorship of Beatrice M. McFall in the Grein Building at the corner of Second and Sycamore Streets. Part of the downtown development plan to create more parking included razing the Grein Buildin, so the Peephole moved over to the corner of Second and Main Streets into a space previously occupied by Wood's Drug Store. By 1973, Norma and Vernon Carter owned the Peephole, and rumors swirled of organized gambling at the bar. Vernon eventually faced fines and indictments about his role in gambling. The Peephole briefly closed in 1986 due to the rising costs of insurance, but it reopened that April and has remained a favorite among downtown patrons, cultivating a community of regulars over the years. At lunchtime, one can see local politicians, lawyers, college students, college professors and community members all enjoying a bowl of chili, a burger and/or a pint of beer. In August 2008, Steve Alsop, Larry "Bubbles" Pollack (The Pub) and Dan DiLegge (of DiLegge's Italian Restaurant) purchased the Peephole and renovated the bar, removing the wood paneling to expose the 1890s bricks. Although some feared the renovation, in an *Evansville Living* article, DiLegge said, "One customer told me, 'I really like what you've done, but you didn't change it.'" The Peephole remains a favorite hole in the wall where local artists showcase their work for sale on the exposed brick.

Peephole. *Author photo.*

PIZZA KING

"If you ask most local residents to describe a Stromboli, you'll hear the same thing—a hoagie bun or split loaf filled with crumbled sausage, pizza sauce and mozzarella cheese and covered in garlic-buttered bread, wrapped and baked in a pizza oven to a state of gooey heavenly deliciousness," wrote *Courier & Press* columnist Aimee Blume in a 2016 article on strombolis. With many locations throughout the Tristate, Pizza King has been in operation since 1956 and is famous for its massive strombolis and pizza, much beloved by many in the region. Pizza King's stroms are so famous that it offers nationwide delivery on dry ice, and copycat "inspired by" recipes are on many Pinterest boards. Founded by Jack and Carol Dillard, the Pizza King chain of restaurants in Evansville and Newburgh is currently owned by Dan and David Nix, owners of Western Ribeye. The Nix family has had a long history in the Evansville restaurant scene—Dan and David's parents, Harold and Carolyn Nix, owned Bockelman's Restaurant and Jacob's Pub.

Recipe for Pizza King–Inspired Stromboli

1 pound milk bulk sausage
1 pound hot Italian sausage (casing removed if using links)
1 large onion, diced
2 cloves garlic, minced
About 30 pepperonis, chopped (stack and chop, makes it easier)
1 cup of your favorite marinara sauce (I used Trader Joe's tomato basil)
3 teaspoons crushed red pepper flakes
6 deli-type rolls
Olive oil
6 sheets of aluminum foil, about 12–14 inches long
1 8-ounce block mozzarella cheese, grated
1 baking sheet

Brown the sausages and onions. Drain any fat from the pan. Add the garlic and chopped pepperoni when the sausage is browned. Add the marinara sauce and red pepper flakes. Stir until thoroughly mixed and heated through. Brush the top and bottom of a deli roll with some good olive oil. Put the sliced deli roll in the middle of a piece of foil and fill with sausage mixture. Put several heaping hands full of cheese on the sausage. Bring the edges of the foil together and roll down to the sandwich and roll the ends up. When all the rolls have been filled and wrapped, place them on a baking sheet and bake in a 350-degree oven for about 20–30 minutes. Remove from the oven and let cool for a few minutes. Unwrap and enjoy.

—http://everydaydonna.blogspot.com/2013/03/midwestern-stromboli-pizza-king-style.html

POUR HOUSE

The physical restaurant may be gone, but the beloved Kitchen Sink pizza from the old Pour House tavern lives on. There were three locations, but the original one on the West Side and the one on Weinbach north of the Lloyd were the most popular. The Pour House was a favorite spot in '70s and '80s but closed in 1986. Owners Tom Groves and his wife, Kathy, originally meant for the bar to be a local nightclub with live music. When that didn't prove profitable, they added pizza after learning a recipe from a Farm Boy product salesman. The Kitchen Sink pizza was the house special—sausage, pepperoni, diced peppers, mushrooms, onions and sliced mozzarella cheese—and it remains the stuff of local legend among Tristate residents. With the advent of social media, locals started talking about their favorite bygone restaurants, and they frequently asked about the Kitchen Sink pizza, which inspired Tom and Kathy to begin making them for other taverns and available to customers by order. They use the same ingredients, purchased from Farm Boy, including the sliced South Alma brand mozzarella. According to a January 2017 *Courier & Press* article, the pizzas are available by order and are on the menu at Franklin Street Tavern and Chilly Willy's Pub on Claremont Avenue. Details about the Kitchen Sink pizza can also be found on social media.

ROCA BAR

The 1618 South Kentucky Avenue establishment known as the Roca Bar opened in 1953 on what was then Highway 41 and was home to the first pizza served in Evansville. Founded by John Rogers and Earl Carter, the name came from combining the first letters of last names to form, but they didn't serve their famous pizza until 1953, when they introduced "a free-form pizza stretched to just right proportions, even if it looked more like a map of New York state," with big bits of ground beef and sausage. The pizza was introduced by chef George Hage of House of Como fame who started as a cook at the Roca Bar. Archie & Clyde's in Newburgh was once associated with the Roca Bar but has since gone independent, and there is also a North Side Evansville location of the Roca Bar that opened in 2010 and serves the same menu of pizzas, the Italian chopped salad, fried appetizers, ice-cold fishbowls of draft beer and a signature margarita, the Rocarita. The famed Italian salad consists

Roca Bar 1945 flood. *Courtesy of the Willard Library Archives.*

Roca Bar. *Author photo.*

of chopped lettuce with ham, pepperoni, egg, tomatoes, green and black olives topped with mixed shredded cheese and Roca Bar Italian dressing. A bright neon sign beckons from the exterior, and the interior of the Roca is old-school nostalgic in both the family dining area and the bar. The Roca Bar menu has numerous specialty pizzas, including chicken barbecue with barbecue sauce, chicken, onions, and jalapeños; Margherita, with olive oil, mozzarella cheese, tomatoes and basil; Round the World special, with beef, sausage, pepperoni, mushrooms, green peppers, onions and tomatoes; Roca Pesto with pesto sauce, chicken, sun-dried tomatoes, spinach and black olives; and the Roca Garden with pesto sauce, broccoli, sun-dried tomatoes, spinach, onions, black olives and artichokes. As with almost all Evansville pizzerias, the crust is thin and crispy like a saltine cracker—just one-sixteenth of an inch thick before baking—secret-recipe sauce spread to the very edges of the crust, cut into squares under heaps of toppings.

THE SLICE

Located adjacent to the University of Evansville, Eric Weber's By the Slice Pizzeria at 2011 Lincoln Avenue has been a neighborhood favorite hole in the wall since 1994. The Slice is a funky little spot in a small strip mall with kitschy décor in the front of the house along several booths and tables for dining—the back is a favorite for UE students with vintage games and pool tables. On any given day, there are about twelve different kinds of specialty pizzas available at the counter for customers to choose from. Among the favorites in regular rotation are the spinach and feta, the chili and the loaded baked potato. Eric also likes to experiment with his pizzas seasonally, often using produce grown at his home. The entire endeavor began as an experiment while Weber was getting his degree at Cornell University according to a 2013 *Courier & Press* interview: "I had a food science class and we started talking about pizza one day and how it's pretty much an edible plate. From the business side, you can put whatever on it as the market dictates, and it's still pizza. You have to have some carbs in there, but otherwise you can do whatever. After that day, I figured pizza was the area I wanted to go into."

SPANKEY'S UNA PIZZA

There have been many iterations of Una pizza throughout Evansville over the years, but one of the favorites is Spankey's Una Pizza on the West Side, first located on Sonntag Avenue before the concept expanded to the Schnuck's Plaza along the Lloyd Expressway. Owner Ryan Huck learned how to make this signature style of thin-crust pizza from working at Stan's Una Pizza for three years before striking out on his own, and he named his location after his family dog, Spankey. Huck also brought some original ideas to the Una style by mixing a sauce that includes a bit of Romano cheese, inspired by Boston pizzas. According to a January 2019 *Courier & Press* article, Huck tried several dozen recipes before creating the perfect sauce and at least a dozen crust recipes before settling on the ones. Spankey's crust is known for being crisp, the spices are mixed by hand and meats are source locally from the Old-Fashioned Butcher Shoppe. While specialty pizzas are on the menu, there are a wide variety of toppings that patrons can use to their imagination, including kraut, dried cranberries and a local favorite—crushed Grippo's chips. Spankey's also has sandwiches with house-made rolls and strombolis, salads and gluten-free and vegan options.

ST. JOE INN

To the northwest of Evansville at 9515 St. Wendel Road is the St. Joe Inn. Once called the Seven Mile House for its distance from Evansville, the St. Joe Inn has roots dating back to 1836. It has been an inn, saloon and hardware store and housed a notary public, justice of the peace and postmaster. The original building burned in the late nineteenth century and was replaced with the current building, which has been owned by Michael Young since 1989. Young claims that the inn is the oldest continuous business in Vanderburgh County. Under his proprietorship, he expanded the spot from a bar that served only burgers and fried chicken to a full menu with steak, seafood and pizza. Favorites include house special chicken wings and the Merkley's German bologna sandwich on house-made bread. Many of the recipes come from Darlene Young, Mike's mother, including potato salad, gravy and bleu cheese dressing. The Youngs' fried chicken is still popular, and they use the same recipe as the Inn's owners in the 1950s.

ST. PHILIP INN

Also on the northwest side of town is the St. Phillip Inn at 11200 Upper Mount Vernon Road. It stakes the claim that it is the oldest bar/restaurant in Posey County, and the original building dates to about 1890, with some claims that the location used to be a Pony Express stop. The menu features fried chicken, pork tenderloin, strombolis and thin-crust pizza. It also has a daily plate lunch special with heaping portions. Among patrons' favorites are the grilled chicken salad, fried fish sandwiches and sides of fried green beans. It was owned and operated for the last twenty years by Matt Riney, who recently listed the establishment for sale in 2019.

STOCKWELL INN

Located on Evansville's East Side between Wesselman Woods and the shops along Green River is the Stockwell Inn at 4001 East Eichel Avenue. Current owner Audrey Christie continues the tradition of plate lunches and tavern favorites in the establishment her parents took over in 1986. With specials every day, the menu includes fried chicken, meat loaf, grilled pork chops, pot roast, open-faced sandwiches and plentiful sides like fried potatoes and baked beans. The bar and restaurant are eclectically decorated with motorsports details and lots of shiny chrome. It also specializes in lunch plates and offers a happy hour from 3:00 p.m. to 6:00 p.m. every weekday.

TALK OF THE TOWN / LOBO LOUNGE

Evansville has some interesting connections to American popular culture, and one of its most famous is the television show *Roseanne*. The creator of the original show, TV producer Matt Williams, used a number of exterior

Talk of the Town/Lobo Lounge. *Author photo.*

shots of places in Evansville for the fictional Lanford, Illinois. This includes the Talk of the Town pizzeria, which appears as the fictional Lobo Lounge. With the reboot of *Roseanne*, the establishment at 1200 Edgar Street officially had its name changed to the Lobo Lounge under the ownership of Robert Redden, Greg Hobgood and Robin Redden Hogbood. On the menu are tavern favorites like strombolis and pizza as well as a full à la carte breakfast menu; it is inspired by Robin's southern heritage from her upbringing in Baton Rouge, Louisiana, including homemade dill ranch dressing. The pizzas are also very popular, including Lobo's take on the West Side–inspired pizza, the Lobo West-Sider, with barbecue sauce, chicken, bacon, jalapeños and mozzarella all topped with crushed BBQ Grippo's. The restaurant also offers a veterans' discount of 50 percent off any order.

TURONI'S

Turoni's was started in 1963 by Jerry Turner, a graduate of North High School who experimented with making pizzas at home before building the iconic Turoni's establishment. The second location on Weinbach Avenue

Turoni's mural. *Author photo.*

Left: Turoni's Pizzeria. *Author photo.*

Below: Turoni's Forget Me Not Inn. *Courtesy of Evansville Vanderburgh Public Library, Evansville Courier & Press Photo Archive.*

took over the historic Forget-Me-Not-Inn in 1990, and there is a Newburgh location as well. Frequently at the top of the *Evansville Courier & Press* Readers' Choice Awards, Turoni's crust and spicy sauce are local and regional legends that many out of towners try to re-create in their own kitchens when they are not able to make the drive into town for their fix. "We try to be consistent," owner Judy Turner told the *Evansville Courier & Press* in September 2019, "We've never changed the pizza. When we started, Jerry and I, we didn't have any money, so Turoni's was decorated like it is right now. We just hung everything on the walls. We'd get a few nice pieces when we could, but I think we were the first to put a conglomeration of things on the walls. The atmosphere is very welcoming and homey. We try to be friendly and make people feel welcome and that's what it is." For three decades, Turoni's has offered thin-crust pizza with a number of gourmet options, including the Cousin Hazel's Famous Meatball with house-made spicy meatballs, garlic, onions and green peppers. Another popular option is the Iron Man, based with pizza sauce topped with garlic, spinach, mozzarella cheese, artichoke hearts and mushrooms. The original location on North Main has murals highlighting local history, and these same designs and motifs can be seen on billboards throughout town and on the menus inside. Since 1996, Turoni's has been a microbrewery as well as a pizzeria, with five craft beers always on menu and seasonal brews as well.

WEINZAPFEL'S TAVERN (ZAP'S TAVERN)

At 3725 St. Philips Road north of Evansville is Weinzapfel's Tavern, now known as Zap's, which has been a community tavern since 1946. Originally owned by the Deig family and now owned by Mike Greenwell and Blake Billman, for over seventy years, the tavern has specialized in great pork chop sandwiches, burgers and house-made soups and chili. In an August 2019 feature in the *Courier & Press*, reporter Aimee Blume suggests that first timers try the kraut ball dip, which has "all the ingredients found in the German appetizer: lots of gooey melted cream cheese, kraut and chunks of sausage topped with a toasty layer of cracker crumbs."

3

Diners, Drive-Ins and Coffeehouses

I n October 2016, *Paste* magazine writer Joan Russell wrote, "The diner is an icon of American culture located in almost every city and town. During most elections political candidates often make a stop at the local diner to meet voters. The diner is a place anyone can go and sit down to eat. Diners were built by many different nationalities using different materials. This melting pot is what produced such a unique well-made building." As more families acquired cars in the 1940s–60s, the drive-in became a popular destination for burgers and shakes. Evansville used to have several unique local and national chain drive-ins and diners, but a few stalwarts remain, with comfort food on the menu for an affordable price. More recently, since the 1990s, coffeehouses have become go-to destinations for quick bites to eat as well as delectable bespoke drinks made to order by knowledgeable baristas serving local fare.

BURGER BANK

To the southeast of Evansville on 1617 South Weinbach Avenue, adjacent to the University South and Presidents neighborhoods, sits a nondescript little 660-square-foot drive-in restaurant, the Burger Bank, in operation since 1962. In an August 17, 1958, *Evansville Courier & Press* advertisement, Evans & England Sales of Morgan Avenue offered an open house viewing of a prefabricated building called the Burger Bank Junior, an eight-by-fourteen-by-eight-foot building with two ten-by-sixteen-foot carports capable of serving "up to 500 cars per operating day" and equipped with everything one would need to start one's own Burger Bank except the food and produce. Financing was available. Renovated in 2009, the Weinbach Burger Bank has served generations of families who have enjoyed sacks of mini burgers at affordable prices—currently priced at ninety-five cents per burger or available by the sack in lots of ten. The most recent owners are Don Falcone and his wife, Gloria, who post their daily half-price specials on social media; these include fried and grilled chicken sandwiches, pork tenderloins, Philly cheesesteaks, patty melts, barbecue and grilled cheese. Sides include fries, tater tots, onion rings, breaded mushrooms, breaded pickles, fried green tomatoes, mozzarella sticks and mac and cheese bites, all in individual or family-size portions.

CAROUSEL

Located south of the Washington Square Mall at 5115 Monroe Avenue, the Carousel Restaurant used to be one of the Merry-Go-Round restaurant locations, a popular family eatery throughout the mid-twentieth century. In 1991, Dilip Patel, an employee of the Merry-Go-Round, bought this location and rebranded the diner as the Carousel. On the menu are family favorites, plate lunches and heaping dinners in a large space that reflects the restaurant's namesake, with carousel décor throughout. The menu is heavy

Carousel Restaurant.
Author photo.

Carousel Restaurant. *Author photo.*

on comfort food, with pork chops, fried chicken, swiss steak, country-fried steak and gravy, beef liver and onions, smoked pork with apples, goulash, spaghetti, ribs and kraut and corned beef with cabbage. The breakfast menu has the classics, including a smoked pork chop with eggs, as well as omelets, sandwiches on fluffy biscuits and a large à la carte menu.

DONUT BANK

Donut Bank Bakery has been an Evansville and Tristate establishment since 1967, offering up all sorts of baked goods and a signature blend of coffee. Owned by the Kempf family, the Donut Bank is consistently on the best of the city lists in both *Evansville Living* and the *Courier & Press*. There are numerous locations around the city, and folks throughout Indiana wish they would expand farther north outside the Tristate so they can have access to their favorites. While mainstay items are donuts, cookies and cakes, the Bank also has healthier alternatives like oatmeal, fit frappes and muffins. Highlander Grog blend coffee is especially popular in the fall and winter months. In any neighborhood in Evansville, one isn't too far from a Donut Bank franchise to get birthday, graduation, baptism, first communion and holiday cakes. Harold and Shirley Kempf opened the first location in 1967 on First Avenue, and they now have nine locations. The farthest north is Princeton, opened in 2008, and the farthest south is Henderson, Kentucky, opened in 2015. While there are frequent calls to expand to Louisville or Indianapolis, the Kempf family is very careful about overextending and believes in quality control. All Donut Bank products are still baked at one location, on Diamond Avenue, and in a 2017 *Courier & Press* article, Harold's son Chris Kempf said, "It's about the quality of the product, first and foremost. People value that for their purchase." From that location, Donut Bank trucks then deliver products to the other locations at around one o'clock in the morning. Any products leftover at the end of the day are donated to local charities, soup kitchens and food banks. While other national chains, like Dunkin' and Krispy Kreme, have entered the region, locals are fiercely loyal and protective of their Donut Bank and have consistently rallied to support their local bakery. Whether it's a cherry Bismark, a maple-iced pecan roll or a sprinkled long john, the Donut Bank always has a fresh supply every morning for an affordable price in a clean and welcoming environment. Tristate residents love that Donut Bank locations are always fast and consistent. Mark Williams said that the Donut Bank is a good place to see friends and have coffee and donuts in the morning and remarked that the chain was one of the first places to go nonsmoking. The favorite of Evansville native and Reitz Memorial High School graduate Michael "Brody" Broshears, assistant vice president for academic success at the University of Southern Indiana, include the traditional glazed, cherry Bismark, fritters and chocolate long john. In an oral history, Brody recalled buying six dozen glazed and six dozen chocolate long johns and selling them for a fundraiser for Reitz Memorial High School Athletics when he was a student. Donut Bank continues to be very active in the community and works with area groups and schools to assist in their fundraising efforts.

EMGE'S DELI

Emge's Deli and Ice Cream has been on Main Street in downtown Evansville since 1974, under the ownership of Jan Howell and, more recently, her co-owner Tracie Jones. A frequent recipient of the *Evansville Courier & Press* Readers' Choice award, the breakfast and lunch spot used to be in a little

Emge's Deli & Ice Cream. *Author photo.*

grocery store spot near the German American Bank before moving to its current location, 206 Main Street. Sandwiches, plate lunches, soups and salads are on the menu. Frequent soup offerings include chili and chicken and dumplings, with four options freshly made daily dependent on the weather. For example, on colder days, options might include loaded baked potato soup, beans and ham or stuffed pepper soup. Comfort foods are Emge's specialty, including Reuben sandwiches and Italian subs as well as grilled cheese, braunschweiger and pimento loaf sandwiches that you can pair with house-made deviled eggs or Amish-style macaroni salad. Plate lunch specials include a popular Thursday staple—a taco salad. Jones and Howell also have a catering side of the business, which includes box lunches for corporate meetings. Many lunch goers love the thinly sliced fried bologna sandwiches.

HONEY + MOON

Near the University of Evansville and in the same plaza as the Slice pizzeria, Jeanie's Gelato and an Asian restaurant named Lincoln Garden is the

Honey+Moon Coffee Co. on the corner of Weinbach and Lincoln Avenues. Owned by Zac Parsons and his wife, Jessica, this recent establishment has become a go-to café for local students as well as young professionals. The first Evansville coffee shop to offer nitro cold brew coffee on tap, it also has a unique food menu that a half-moon tortilla sandwich, crescent moon croissants and signature bubble waffles. The owners also have recently expanded their operations to include a downtown location. The coffee is roasted locally, and the locations frequently have specialty brews that reflect local history or events, including the Rami Malek macchiato, made with popcorn syrup, milk, espresso and caramel, that celebrated the University of Evansville graduate's Oscar win. Honey+Moon is part of a recent local trend toward revitalizing neighborhoods and the Evansville downtown with cafés that feature local artists and food as well as supporting other ventures in town. To that end, Parsons has collaborated with a newer Evansville brewery, Myriad, located in the old McCurdy Hotel along the Evansville riverfront to provide cold brew for their latest beers.

LIC'S DELI & ICE CREAM

Another establishment that one can find in many neighborhoods around the Tristate are the pastel buildings of Lic's, an acronym of Lloyd's Ice Cream Shoppes, established in 1950 with all house-made ice creams, sandwiches, soups and specialty desserts. While the desserts and hand-packed quarts of ice cream are much beloved, the menu also includes Angus beef cheeseburgers, grilled cheese sandwiches with spicy chili and, on the lighter side, soups of the day and an apple/praline salad with house-made vinaigrette. Lic's has eight locations from Vincennes in the north to Owensboro to the southeast. Don Smith bought the business in 1963, and his daughter Kara Combs is the current director of marketing—it was her grandmother who created the house vinaigrette, a sweet Italian variation, which can also be purchased by the pint. All of the sandwich bread and cakes are baked at a downtown production facility and delivered, except Vincennes and Owensboro, which receive unbaked dough that they bake on site to ensure freshness. None of the Lic's bread has any preservatives. Chococremes are quite the treat: bite-size ice cream balls in vanilla bean, Dutch chocolate, butter pecan, black cherry or custom flavor dipped in chocolate. Chococremes are available by the dish, pint or quart. Lic's has a disclaimer, warning, "May be Habit

Forming!" You can also order a Sundae Party with the ice cream flavor of your choice, toppings, nuts, candies, dishes and spoon to create your own sundaes, available for delivery or carryout.

MERRY-GO-ROUND

Merry-Go-Round opened in June 1948, and its website boasts that with "neon, curb girls, and convertibles, this place was hopping from the beginning. Virgil Syerup's Merry-Go-Round opened first in June 1948 on Old Highway 41 with drive-in service and carhops serving what would become a local delicacy, the Dilly Burger. When the mid-sixties rolled around an addition to the Merry-Go-Round Restaurant and a new menu, aimed at family dining, was born. Full sit-down service with super plate lunches and great

Merry-Go-Round. *Courtesy of the University of Southern Indiana.*

sandwiches were the order of the day." In 1966, the location and the menu expanded to include plate lunches as well as a full sit-down service of family-friendly comfort foods. Eric Raeber, an employee since 1970, bought the establishment in 1982, and he and his family continue to keep the tradition alive. His son, Cam, is the head chef, and Eric's wife, Natalie, is known for her homemade pies and salads. The Merry-Go-Round recently celebrated its sixty-fifth anniversary with record crowds during a customer appreciation week—patrons had many stories to share about their memories. This restaurant is still in business; the photos shown here include a new 1960s dining room.

OLD MILL

Located at 5031 New Harmony Road since 1936, the Old Mill serves up family-style dinners that include a choice of fried chicken, honey-roasted ham or roast beef served with mashed potatoes, cream gravy, green beans, sweet corn, German coleslaw and homemade rolls as well as a full menu of options. Friday through Sunday, the Old Mill offers a large seafood buffet. The main dining is available for private events for up to four hundred people, and an adjacent party room can hold up to three hundred guests.

PENNY LANE

Penny Lane, in Haynie's Corner adjacent to downtown Evansville, has been the go-to coffeehouse in the historic district since 2000. Local art adorns the walls, and on the menu are eclectic organic and vegan dishes as well as handcrafted coffee and tea drinks. It also happens to be in a historic building that used to house a pharmacy owned by Annie Fellows Johnston and her husband, William L. Johnston. Annie Fellows Johnston was a famous Evansville resident whose younger sister was the famous Evansville progressive feminist Albion Fellows Bacon. Annie took up writing professionally after the death of her husband, and her works are globally known, especially the Little Colonel series (1896) which inspired a 1935 Shirley Temple movie. Penny Lane has also been the stumping spot

Penny Lane Coffeehouse. *Author photo.*

for local and national politicians, including former president Bill Clinton. On the menu are daily specialty coffee concoctions, smoothies, teas and tasty treats, including sandwiches and quiches. Breakfast items tend toward fried egg sandwiches on flaky croissants or fluffy muffins, as well as biscuits and gravy. Gluten-free, vegan and vegetarian options are available.

PIE PAN

On the North Side of town since 1978, the Pie Pan underwent a total renovation in 2017 under new owners Jackie Weil, Gary Wilson and two other local investors. Weil worked for owner Libby Lear for thirteen years before beginning this new chapter of the Pie Pan's history. For the most part, however, the menu remains unchanged, with familiar favorites chicken and dressing, meatloaf and, of course, pies. It is a favorite breakfast spot with a full menu that includes quiche. It is also a stumping ground for political leaders, local and national, including former U.S. senator Joe Donnelly and 2016 presidential hopeful Ted Cruz. The pies are the highlight with over thirty different house-made options to choose from, including pumpkin, country apple, cherry, coconut cream and the popular rhubarb. Local radio station 106.1 KIIS FM featured the Pie Pan in its March 2019 list of most underrated restaurants, recommending the "amazing breakfasts."

Pie Pan Chess Pie

12 eggs
3 pounds sugar
4 tablespoons cornmeal
8 ounces margarine
6 cups half-and-half
Pinch of salt
4 teaspoons vanilla
4 pie shells

Mix all ingredients. Pour in four pie shells. Bake at 350 degrees until firm and golden brown—about 40 to 45 minutes.

Tillie Bockelman's Cheesecake

1 cup graham cracker crumbs
3 tablespoons sugar
3 tablespoons margarine, melted
3 (8-ounce) packages cream cheese, softened
½ cup sugar
2 tablespoons flour
3 eggs
2 tablespoons milk
1 teaspoon vanilla
21 ounces cherry pie filling

Combine crumbs, sugar and margarine. Press onto bottom of 9-inch springform pan. Bake at 325 degrees for 10 minutes. Then increase oven to 450 degrees.

Combine softened cream cheese, sugar and flour, mixing at medium speed with electric mixer until well blended. Add eggs, one at a time; mix well after each egg is added. Blend in milk and vanilla. Pour mixture over crust. Bake at 450 degrees for 10 minutes. Reduce oven temperature to 250 degrees. Continue baking for 25 to 35 minutes. Cool before removing rim of pan. Before serving, top with pie filling. Makes 1 cheesecake.

—*Evansville Press*, "The Pie Pan," October 20, 1982

RIVER CITY COFFEE & GOODS

Part of the key players in the revitalization of Evansville's downtown Main Street are Clint and Heather Vaught. They own River City Mercantile, where they house a bespoke coffee shop alongside offerings from local and regional artisans, including handmade soaps by 6th Street Soapery in Haynie's Corner, embroidered tea towels by Hat & Rabbit and Evansville-centric merchandise designed by Heather as part of her Steadfast Media

River City Coffee & Goods. *Author photo.*

label. They source their coffee beans from Quills Coffee in Louisville, an establishment that they have visited frequently to attend classes and train for their shop. Located just off the corner of Third and Main, the Vaughts' opened River City in 2016 in a 130-year-old building, where they also have created a space for Clint's tattoo museum and shop. On the coffee side of the business they offer chai, espresso, pour over, specialty drinks with house-made syrups and an assortment of locally made baked goods, including vegan muffins and Pop-Tarts.

ZESTO'S

L.A.M. Phelan was an inventor and head of the Taylor Freezer Corporation who in 1945 created the Zest-O-Mat frozen custard machine. The first Zesto Drive-In with contracted agreements to use the Zest-O-Mat machines originated in Jefferson City, Missouri, in 1948—other franchises opened primarily in the Midwest and the South throughout the 1950s. It was originally known as Zesto Drive-In and featured ice cream and frozen

Zesto. *Courtesy of the Willard Library Archives.*

custard. Evansville has two locations, including one on Riverside Drive along the southeast side of town and one on Franklin on the near North Side. All Zesto's are independently owned and operated, and each has its own take on familiar drive in staples—greasy burgers, breaded pork tenderloins and deep-fried onion rings are always popular. In the summertime, lines crowd around the Riverside location custard cones twirled with flavor bursts, a fruity twist in a technicolor rainbow of options. The "Family Pack" consists of four jumbo cheeseburgers, family-size fries, choice of large onion rings or medium poppers all for just $13.25. In a 2007 feature in *Evansville Living*, reporter Jesse Southerland quipped, "When you bite into a pork tenderloin at the Zesto Drive-In (102 W. Franklin St.), any chance you had at a healthy meal vanishes when the mayonnaise-covered shredded lettuce plops off the sandwich and onto your lap. But, what the sandwich lacks in health, it makes up for in size, taste, and price....The tenderloin—a boneless, tender slice of lean meat—comes in two sizes at Zesto: the regular and the giant. The latter is nearly as large as your face." The Riverside location recently celebrated sixty-seven years with a March 2019 feature in the *Courier & Press*. Owner Dan Hardesty shared that folks drive in from all over the Tristate: "We have people from Boonville (or) Henderson, down in Kentucky that will pop in and say, 'we drove all the way from so and so.' We still do everything the same as we always did, so it's the old-fashioned things people like, and they find it fascinating and interesting."

4
International and Traditional Cuisines

International restaurants, often owned by immigrants to the United States, have a long tradition in American history. These eateries are pathways to the American dream, offering delectable and unique dishes that can change the landscape of the communities they live in. Evansville's connection to Chinese and Italian cuisine dates back to the early twentieth century but more recent eateries have expanded the community palate for Middle Eastern, Mediterranean, Southeast Asian, Mexican and pan-fusion internationally inspired options. This chapter engages with both international fare and traditional midwestern cuisines like Evansville's take on barbecue. While our Kentucky neighbor to the southeast, Owensboro, has laid claim to being a barbecue capital, spots like Marx and Wolf's have kept generations of families coming back for their delightful barbecue traditions and homestyle fare.

ACROPOLIS

At 501 North Green River Road, Doros and Ellada Hadjisavva opened their Acropolis restaurant with Ellada's brother George Yerolemou in 1999. A native of Cyprus, Doros spoke recently in September 2019 with the *Courier & Press*: "Our 20-year anniversary is coming up soon. We have visibility and a good location, and Ellada and I are very active in the business. Acropolis is Doros and Ellada, and we are Acropolis. We believe that if we're going to be in

Acropolis. *Author photo.*

the community we want to be involved in it, so we do the charity functions and do the donations. I think that helps us the most. Having a restaurant is not just opening the doors at 11 a.m. and waiting. We've adjusted the menu over the years to cater to Evansville's tastes. To maintain a big restaurant like this, you have to bring a big crowd, so we offer the steaks, chops, a cheeseburger and we have increased to 160 whiskeys and Bourbons so now we have people come in just for the bar." The extensive menu at Acropolis restaurant has delicious authentic Greek- and American-inspired dishes such as gyro platters; moussaka with sliced eggplant, zucchini, potatoes and choice ground beef covered with bechamel sauce; and Chicken Lemonati with chicken breast sautéed in mushrooms, artichokes, Greek seasonings and tomatoes in a creamy lemon sauce served over rice or pasta. The Acropolis website also includes a directory of Greek recipes and articles of interest. Acropolis also has a thriving catering business both on location and at area facilities, including the picturesque Old Post Office downtown.

ANGELO'S

Located at 305 Main Street since 1993, Angelo's is a popular downtown staple specializing in old-school Italian cuisine like Chicken Marsala,

Angelo's. *Author photo.*

Veal Parmigiano, Shrimp Scampi and traditional pasta dishes. A 2014 *Evansville Living* feature recommended that patrons "Dine on the Chicken ala Crema, a recipe accidentally made when owner Angelo Jawabreh poured Alfredo sauce over chicken Marsala. The dish found a life at the restaurant among other authentic favorites." The beautifully decorated Italy-inspired Gondola Room is available for reservation for larger parties. Cannoli, house-made tiramisu, cheesecake and silk pies are available for dessert.

CANTON INN

The Canton Inn is a continuation of the influence of Cantonese chefs who first worked in the tristate at F's Steakhouse. The first location opened in December 1984 after Yim Seto and his father, Shum, decide to open their own restaurant. It was the first Chinese buffet in Evansville, and the owners expanded the Canton Inn to a bigger location in May 2000 at 947 North Park Drive. Yim worked for F's for three years, while his father cooked there for over twenty years before they decided it was time for their own spot focusing on traditional Cantonese dishes like chow mein, lo mein and sweet-and-sour pork. Their sweet-and-sour sauce is based on traditional Hong Kong and Cantonese dishes made with tomato, pineapple and turnips. They also have American favorites like crab rangoon. Cantonese dishes are chicken stock–based, and the Setos make their broth in-house. In a September 2019 *Courier & Press* article, Yim Seto offered some of their secrets to success, "Everything we use is fresh," said Seto. "In the morning we get the chicken bones boiling into stock. We use it to make the soup first, then we keep it boiling all day to use in the dishes. We don't add any vegetables, just the bones, for the pure flavor. It has to be fresh. We don't keep anything overnight. We also don't use anything in a can. We chop the broccoli and bok choy and other vegetables every day." Favorite dishes for many diners include the fried rices, lo mein, wor mein and the egg drop soup. One of their most popular menu dishes is the war sue gai, which is a breaded chicken breast that is sliced and coated with a brown gravy made from soy sauce, white pepper and sesame oil.

DILEGGE'S

Since 1987, DiLegge's on North Main Street has been a family tradition that showcases the culinary traditions of their ancestry in Abruzzi, Italy. Housed in a building that is at least a century old, it's a family affair that has involved Dan DiLegge and his sisters, their mother, at least one aunt and numerous cousins, nieces and nephews. Their house-made ragu is the base of a number of their dishes on their hearty menu of pastas. A unique dish to try is the hot-and-spicy vegetables pasta, which has roasted peppers, mushrooms, sun-dried tomatoes, zucchini, yellow squash and onions in a spicy garlic olive oil sauce, lightly dusted with Parmesan cheese. Dan DiLegge began as a manager of the Knights of Columbus on Maryland Street, where he began offering Italian nights before deciding to ask his family to help him build their own place; his sister Gina was very involved from day one. DiLegge's features original family recipes, including sausage and meatballs, and claims to be the first to feature baked ziti and fettucine alfredo on the menu in the Evansville region. Lasagne with meatballs, sausages and three cheeses is a popular dish, as is baked eggplant, chicken or veal parmesan, and an array of pastas—spaghetti, rigatoni, mostaccioli, manicotti and ziti. In a 1988 *Courier & Press* article on regional sandwiches, Dan DiLegge shared the makings of an Italian grinder.

Italian Grinder Hoagie

About 8 ounces tomato sauce
2 hoagie buns, buttered and partially baked
½ pound Italian meatballs or sausage
½ cup grated Parmesan cheese
4 slices provolone cheese
Hot giardiniera mix or mild fried peppers
Garlic butter

Divide tomato sauce between bottoms of two partially baked hoagie buns. Top with meatballs or sausage. Sprinkle with grated Parmesan cheese. Add two pieces of sliced provolone cheese to each hoagie bottom. Add hot giardiniera mix or mild fried peppers, to taste. Cover sandwich with top of bun. Baste top of bun with butter seasoned with garlic. Bake in a 350-degree oven for about 15 minutes. Serves 2–4.

—*Evansville Courier*, "What's Your Favorite Sandwich", June 19, 1988

When recently asked about their long history by the *Courier & Press* in August 2019, "Good food, good portions, good service and reasonable prices," owner Dan DiLegge summed up. "People come in and have one meal, then take home leftovers and have another meal. Sometimes people say they had two more meals. We don't take short cuts and never have. My sister Gina DiLegge Mueller is the chef, and my niece Emily runs the banquet room and does a good job, it stays booked. Family has been an integral part of the restaurant. We've grown and expanded. We

DiLegge's. *Author photo.*

added the banquet room 10 years ago and opened the garden patio in 2013 and really work on having beautiful landscaping and making it one of the nicest places in town for outdoor dining."

GERST HAUS

At the heart of the Franklin Street renaissance is the Gerst Haus Bavarian restaurant at 2100 West Franklin Street, which opened in 1999 and is owned by Jim and Jerry Chandler. The building itself has a long history; it opened in 1890 as the Rosenberger's wholesale grocery before becoming the Heldt & Voelker hardware store in 1925. Most of the building has remained the same over the years—the ceiling, floors, ladder against the east wall and stage area were all part of the older establishments. The Gerst Haus is a satellite of a now-shuttered Nashville restaurant that used to brew the signature Gerst Amber beer. The beer selection is legendary, with a collection of imported and domestic beers served in frozen fishbowls or pints. Their bar comes from a closed tavern called the Fortune Teller in St. Louis. The menu includes a section of German and American foods. On the European heritage side,

Above: Gerst Haus postcard street view. *Courtesy of the University of Southern Indiana.*

Left: Gerst Haus Westside Nut Club Squirrel. *Author photo.*

Gerst Haus storefront. *Author photo.*

the dishes favor wiener schnitzel, goulash, bratwurst, Hungarian paprikash and sauerbraten. Appetizers include the Gerst sampler, which consists of fried ham rolls, fried kraut balls, potato pancakes and fried oyster rolls. The traditional combination dinner consists of choice of any three of the following: bratwurst, kasseler rippchen, knackwurst, kielbasa, beef stroganoff, schnitzel, goulash and sauerbraten, plus a choice of two sides and freshly baked rye bread.

The Gerst Haus recently celebrated a twentieth anniversary, and the *Courier & Press* sat down with management (manager Paul Ankenbrand, dining room manager Beth Ann Reisinger, kitchen manager Romie Kimbrell and assistant kitchen manager Sam Cowgill) to talk about fun facts. These included musings on the specialty dishes, including the chicken tortilla soup, decidedly not German but a much beloved option served every Wednesday. Every weekend, the Gerst serves about eighty pounds of pork knuckles with kraut. One hundred heads of red cabbage are chopped a week for the rott trohl with sugar, red apple and spices. The German bologna, bratwurst, knackwurst, smoked mettwurst and Berliner mett are a house recipe and all made by Dewig's in Haubstadt. Every two days, the staff makes eleven gallons of beef stroganoff, a recipe for which follows.

Beef Stroganoff

2½ pounds inside rounds, diced in 1-inch squares
1½ cups diced yellow onion
½ pound butter
1½ teaspoons white pepper
4 cups flour
1 quart water
¼ pound beef base
¼ pound sour cream
¼ cup red wine
½-inch egg noodles

Combine the beef round, onions, butter and pepper and let simmer for one hour. Add 4 cups of flour. Mix in water, beef base, sour cream and red wine. Serve over egg noodles.

—http://evansvilledining.com/articles/2008/beef-stroganoff.aspx

Apple Cobbler

1 cup water
2 cups sugar
1 cup heavy cream
6 tablespoons cinnamon
¼ cup cornstarch
1 dozen peeled Granny Smith apples, cored and sliced

Crust
1 cup milk
1 cup flour
1 cup sugar

Put water in saucepan; add sugar and stir until it dissolves. Add cream and cinnamon and stir. Add corn starch and stir until it becomes a syrup. Mix crust ingredients well and place in bottom of 6-by-8-inch pan. Put apples on top, then cover with sauce. Cook at 350 for 30 minutes. Dough will rise through and around the crust.

Rice Pilaf

2 cups long-grain white rice
4 cups water
5 tablespoons butter
½ teaspoon chopped garlic
½ green bell pepper, diced
¼ cup diced celery
½ fresh tomato, diced

Bring rice and water to a boil (about 20 minutes); let simmer and set aside. Put butter and chopped garlic in sauté pan; simmer for a minute or two. Add peppers, celery and tomatoes. Toss. Simmer another two minutes and add rice. Toss again, and then serve.

Baked Cinnamon Apples

1 cup water
2 cups sugar
1 cup heavy cream
6 tablespoons cinnamon
¼ cup cornstarch
1 dozen unpeeled Granny Smith apples, cored and sliced

Put water in pan; add sugar and stir until it dissolves. Add cream and cinnamon and stir. Add corn starch and stir until it becomes a syrup. Add apples; cook 10 to 15 minutes, or until soft.

Stuffed Pork Tenderloin

½ cup self-rising flour
½ cup sugar
2 cups self-rising cornmeal
¼ celery stalk, diced
1 cup buttermilk
2-pound pork tenderloin
¼ cup water
¼ cup canola oil

Place flour, sugar, cornmeal, celery and buttermilk in bowl and mix well. Let it rise and fall twice (about 10 to 15 minutes). Bake at 350 degrees in 6-by-8-inch pan until it's cornbread consistency, about 20 minutes. Chop in food processor; add water until it becomes doughy again.

Butterfly tenderloin; lay it flat. Place cornbread in center of pork loin and roll up pork loin. Using cooking string, tie ends and tie off every two inches.

In a sauté pan, add canola oil and sear tenderloin. Put in baking pan and cook at 350 degrees for 45 minutes to 1 hour, or until internal temperature is 190 degrees.

To plate, remove strings and slice into half-inch medallions. Serve with baked apples and rice pilaf.

—*Evansville Courier & Press*, "Chef's Challenge: Gerst Haus Recipes," April 23, 2008

THE WEST SIDE NUT CLUB formed in 1921 to sponsor events for the betterment of the West Side, including the yearly weeklong Fall Festival. Oak trees have a long symbolic history to those of Germanic heritage, and the acorn is the West Side Nut Club. A large carved squirrel and acorn sit right outside the Gerst Haus.

JIMMY JENG'S SZECHWAN

Known throughout its two-decade history as Jimmy Jeng's, for a short time as Gao's, now simply Szechwan Restaurant, this specialty Chinese eatery at 669 North Green River Road offers up a tantalizing selection of Szechwan province delights as well as familiar favorites on the robust menu. The tradition of red chili spice is an important component, and any recipe can be altered to diners' specific wishes to the level of heat or spiciness that they prefer. Traditional Szechwan-inspired dishes familiar to American diners include kung pao chicken, but adventurous diners can also order off the more authentic Chinese menu, which is available upon request. Popular items at the restaurant include apple shrimp, prawns with lychee, crazy garlic beef with broccoli, honey sesame bee and vegetable foo young.

The restaurant got its start under the leadership of Jimmy Jeng, who built a loyal customer base with his flavorful menu, which included Szechwan dumplings in a sweet and spicy sauce and spicy scallops in a black bean sauce served with baby bok choy. He had the help of a Chaowu Dong, a master Szechwan chef, and Dong's wife, Jing Li. Dong and Li are from Chengdu City, the capital of the Szechwan province, and had a long history

Szechwan. *Author photo.*

in the culinary and hospitality business before coming to Evansville in 2001 to work with Jimmy Jeng. Dong helped establish a much-beloved culinary tradition and worked for Jeng until 2013, when Dong moved to California for work. Jimmy Jeng retired in 2015, and for a short time, Jimmy Gao took over the restaurant until Dong returned to take over the establishment with his wife, keeping many of the favorites on the menu while adding a few new dishes, including the Chengdu Twice Cooked Pork.

LA CAMPIRANA

While there are many Mexican restaurants around the Tristate, the most authentic taco shop is owned by Abraham Brown and Ezequiel Campos, La Campirana, at 724 North Burkhart Road. La Campirana means "from the countryside," which explains a bit of the mission behind the restaurant, that everything served is fresh and authentic. Campos had experience as manager at the West Side Los Bravos restaurant. The two desired real Mexican tacos and had been in the habit of driving to Indianapolis or Nashville in order to have real Mexican-style dishes before they decided to pool their savings and build their own business. La Campirana began as a little shop in 2015 in the Washington Square Mall's food court before the owners expanded to their current location. Almost immediately, La Campirana was a hit with the local Latino community and became destination for foodies desiring authentic simple dishes. On the menu are street tacos, quesadillas, flautas, caldo de res, birria and tortas. Birria is a popular dish made from shredded marinated rib meat served in a spicy sauce with sides of rice, fresh cilantro, chopped onions and house-made corn or flour tortillas. Alambres is another favorite dish made with the diner's choice of meat served with seared peppers and onions covered in Chihuahua cheese. La Campirana also offers fresh jugos (juices), aquas frescas, horchata and smoothies as well as pastries and paletas (popsicles). Recently, in conjunction with the Latino community, the restaurant sponsored a Día de los Muertos event out at the Angel Mounds historic site with vendors, artisans and lectures on the history of the celebration of ancestors.

MANNA

Located in what was once a Lee's Chicken at 2913 Lincoln Avenue since 2009, Manna is a favorite on the near East Side and is owned by Damascus, Syria native Amjad Manna and his wife, Kristi. Amjad is the nephew of Raffi Manna, who once owned the popular Italian restaurant Raffi's Restaurant on North Burkhardt Road and now owns the Mediterranean-inspired Oasis Café on Virginia Street. Amjad began working with his uncle at Raffi's in 1997 and is a graduate of the University of Southern Indiana. Specializing in Middle Eastern appetizers, salads, entrées and desserts, the affordable menu at Manna also has gluten-free, vegetarian and vegan options. Diners can fill fluffy pita with creamy house-made hummus and baba ganouj (roasted eggplant dip)—a rainbow of colors on each plate. Stuffed grape leaves filled with rice, onion, tomatoes, parsley and spices can be accompanied by fried falafels with a side salad of chopped romaine, cucumbers, tomatoes, green onions and olive oil dressing. From the website, "Here at the Manna Mediterranean Grill, we prepare fresh, flavorful and fast meals inspired from the regions surrounding the Mediterranean Sea. This region is known all over the world for their culinary style using fresh lemons, exotic spices and pure olive oil. The careful selection of fresh vegetables, grains, legumes and meats infused with the spices and culinary style of the Mediterranean makes these entrees mouth-watering and memorable." Popular dishes include beef, lamb or chicken kabobs and chicken shawarma.

MARX BBQ

A historic Evansville West Side icon, Marx Barbecue at 3119 West Maryland Street has been serving generations of tristate families. Elmer Marx established the business in 1954, and it remains a family affair after Elmer's brother Roy took over and is now run by Tony Marx, Roy's grandson. Marx Barbecue is beloved for its original recipe tomato-based barbecue sauce slathered on pulled pork, chicken and ribs. The restaurant has an extensive catering business that offers whole smoked hogs, pulled pork, barbecued chicken, sliced ham, smoked turkey and fried chicken, as well as popular side items. The kitchen frequently preps the most recent menu item, the pork grenade, for events such as the West Side Nut Club Fall Festival. The pork grenade, which will also be available at the Hilltop Inn, is house-made pork sausage mixed with ground pulled pork, wrapped with two slices of bacon, then smoked and topped with sweet and sassy barbecue sauce, a recipe from Tony's dad. The original barbecue sauce was developed back in 1954 and is made in a couple forty-five-gallon batches every week. The sweet and sassy barbecue sauce is made in batches by Farm Boy. Side items include American and German potato salads as well as macaroni salad and coleslaw. All desserts, including coconut pies and Ski pies, are made in-house. House-made soups are very popular as well, available for takeout by the quart, especially the burgoo. And if you're taking some to go, be sure to grab a bag of chocolate chip cookies, too good to skip. The Ski pies are a more recent addition. Beginning in 2015, Marx began offering a twist on the regional favorite, bottled in Evansville at the Royal Crown Bottling Company and affectionately known as West Side water. The citrus soda is a base for a tart icebox pie. While the Marx recipe is a family secret, Ski recently published its own variation, as follows.

Ski Pie

1 pie crust
1 box lemon pudding
1 can Ski Citrus Soda
Whipped cream

Bake crust according to directions. Prep pudding. Add 1 can Ski to pudding. Pour into pie crust. Refrigerate for ½ to 1 hour before serving. Top with whipped cream.

—https://wkdq.com/how-to-make-ski-pie.

MA.T.888

MA.T.888 China Bistro opened in 2014 as an upscale restaurant serving exquisite Chinese fare in a beautiful space decorated with fresh flowers and Asian sculptures. Owner Ling Ma is from the Canton province of China, and she owns the restaurant with her husband, Tian Ma, whose grandfather first came to the Evansville area. The family opened its first restaurant in Mount Carmel, Illinois, in the early 1980s before they opened Mandarin Garden in the mid-1990s and the China Bistro in 2007. The Ma stands for the family name, T is for Tang and 888 is considered the luckiest combination of numbers in China. The restaurant serves Cantonese, Hunan and Szechwan cuisines and is located in a large space at 5636 Vogel Road. MA.T.888 also has takeout options, including the Royal Queen dinner, which consists of pork spring roll, a choice between hot and sour or egg drop soup, and a choice of two dishes: sweet and sour chicken, emerald jade chicken spicy garlic pork, Mongolian beef (spicy), shrimp with vegetables, Eight Treasure Delight or General Tso's chicken (spicy). Strawberry Cream Delight is a featured dessert. The Royal King Dinner includes the same appetizers, soup and dessert, but the main dish options change to cashew chicken, orange chicken (spicy), ginger pork, sesame beef (spicy), crispy honey shrimp (spicy), chicken with double mushroom or beef with vegetables. The restaurant recently expanded to include the Domo Sushi Bar and Ramen House. The Domo is under chef Marvin Abadacio, a native of the Philippines who began working for Nagasaki Inn in 2003 and then was a part owner of

MA.T.888. *Author photo.*

Zuki Japanese restaurants before partnering with Ling Ma of MA.T.888. A highlight of Domo is a Tristate tradition of complex sushi rolls based on American tastes that Abadacio began creating first at Nagasaki. For traditionalists, there is also the option of omakase, or chef's choice, which is a more authentic version. Another foodie highlight are the bowls of ramen: shoyu ramen with soy sauce–based broth, miso ramen with soybean broth and tonkotsu ramen with a pork bone broth. All of these bowls are then topped with chasu pork belly, pork rib with meat, medium-boiled egg, seaweed and scallions. For lunch patrons, there is also an option of the traditional bento box with salad, miso, yakisoba noodles, teriyaki chicken and a choice of sushi—sashimi, nigiri or marinated tuna.

PANGEA

International fusion cuisine is the driving theme behind Pangea Kitchen at 111 South Green River Road, Suite E, in the Brinker's Plaza. Pangea Kitchen, a "global soul food market," is the dream of Randy Hobson, who spent twenty-five years working for Berry Plastics, which afforded him the opportunity to travel all over the United States and the world. He experienced the diversity of food options in large cities and wanted to bring some of those experiences to Evansville. Thus, when he retired, he opened Pangea in 2016. The menu is eclectic, with two seemingly disparate but remarkably complementary ethnic cuisines at the forefront: Thai and Italian. Simple authentic ingredients and processes are at the heart of dishes, and Hobson imports ingredients from all over the world to make many of the products in-house according to time-honored recipes. Thai options include Pad Ke Mao, or drunken noodles, which customers can add a meat to. Thai dishes are created by Chef Wanphen McDonald, who trained at the Royal Thai School of Culinary Arts in Bangkok. On occasion, ramen noodle bowls are offered in a popup night. Pangea is one of the few American restaurants certified to offer authentic Neapolitan pizza in the old-style tradition. The True Neapolitan Pizza Association (Associazione Verace Pizza napoletana or AVPN) has certified Pangea as an official restaurant that serves True Neapolitan Pizza (Vera Pizza Napoletana), a designation that fewer than eight hundred restaurants have worldwide. These traditional pies also have a regional flavor to them—for example, the Hot Don references an old car commercial that many Tristaters grew up with. And it is spicy! The pie is made with milled San Marzano tomato, Italian sausage, spicy soppressata, sambal Calabrian chilies and house-made mozzarella, and it is drizzled with extra virgin olive oil. On the white pie side of the menu is the popular pancetta option with house-made mozzarella, pancetta, brussels sprouts, basil, ricotta and parmigiana, drizzled with balsamic vinaigrette glaze. If diners desire a thick deep-dish option, the Pangea bakers are also trained in Detroit style, including another spicy dish, the Diavola. This pie is made with red sauce, brick cheese, house-made mozzarella with spicy sausage, hot soppressata, sambal, Calabrian chilies and parmesan and drizzled with garlic olive oil. If diners have any appetite left, they can take a peek at the gelato and pastry bar with decadent options like cannoli, macarons and tarts prepared by Sarah Bruggeman. The minds behind Pangea are also in the process of developing another project in downtown Evansville in the former National Biscuit Company factory built in 1889. This is a collaboration with Mike Martin of Architectural Renovators, who was responsible for the Greyhound Station transformation into Bru Burger (see chapter 5).

SHING LEE

Shing Lee sits at 215 Main Street and has withstood the tests of time, fires and food trends. Forced to close after a 1997 fire and another in 2016, Ling Jung and her husband, Foo Shung "Frankie," were resilient about twice reopening after extensive renovations and continuing their legacy in Evansville, which they've called home since 1971. Like many of the Chinese restaurants in town, Shing Lee has connections to F's Steakhouse. Frankie Jung came to F's to work with his uncle John Chong and attend the University of Evansville. Chong eventually left F's to open the House of Chong, and Jung and his wife, Ling, opened Shing Lee with Jung's father, Chew Fon Jung. A 1978 *Courier & Press* review noted the attention to decorative detail that "made dining a pleasure," with fine dining in the tradition of "Old China." The renovated space maintains that tradition with opulent decorations and a menu that has always focused on traditional Cantonese-style foods like sesame chicken or sweet and sour chicken served with fresh vegetables. As Linda Negro, a *Courier & Press* food critic and reviewer, opined in a 2004 column, "In this day of gargantuan mega buffets, it's nice to pull up to a table and have a dish prepared specifically for you. The meals at Shing Lee will be made to your specifications." Chicken chow mein is a popular dish

Above: Shing Lee Restaurant.
Author photo.

Left: Shing Lee Restaurant logo.
Author photo.

served with onions, celery, water chestnuts and bean sprouts, along with white rice and chow mein noodles. All dishes are served with a cup of egg drop soup. One of the unique characteristics of the Shing Lee menu is that all dishes are customizable according to diner preferences by request. In a 2007 *Courier & Press* restaurant review, owner Ling Jung quipped, "Our restaurant is so old, people come and tell us what to do." Shing Lee reopened along Main Street in 2018, and *Evansville Living* covered its reopening: "The sesame chicken remains the restaurant's most popular and requested dish, although the sweet and sour wonton and fried rice also are popular. Frankie says they have been overwhelmed with the excitement of the community since reopening and already have welcomed back many of their previous regulars." With the long wait over, Shing Lee seeks to reclaim their top spot as a favorite takeout and dine-in establishment.

SMITTY'S

The owners of the Gerst Haus, Jim and Jerry Chandler, are also the proprietors of Smitty's Italian Steakhouse at 2109 West Franklin Street, which they opened in 2001. Named after an old bar on the corner of Franklin and Main Streets, the original Smitty's lives on, as the Chandlers transported the wooden back bar from that location to their new restaurant. The made-from-scratch menu includes chicken or veal marsala and lasagna, but customer favorites are the variety of steaks followed up with a piece of Italian cream cake or bread pudding with praline sauce. Romie Kimbrell is the executive chef, and he has worked for the Chandlers in their restaurants for over two decades. All steaks are from corn-fed midwestern beef. The

Smitty's Italian Steakhouse.
Author photo.

restaurant atmosphere is inspired by Italian country food and the farm-to-table movement, with regional ingredients and dishes made to order. From the website, "Our core belief: great food need not be elaborate or overwrought, but rather fresh, uncomplicated and well executed in order to get out of the way of the ingredients and find the joy in their innate flavors and qualities."

TAJ MAHAL

Located at 900 Tutor Lane #101, Taj Mahal is a popular Indian buffet with full menu options for dine-in and takeout on the East Side off North Burkhardt Road. The buffet offers curries, biryani and other Indian classics. While the main dish offerings vary, there are always pans filled with naan bread to go alongside items like chicken tikka masala, consisting of roasted chicken pieces cooked in creamy honey tomato sauce, or Saag Paneer, made from fried cottage cheese cubes cooked in spinach and spices. Popular appetizers include the vegetable samosas, a simple dish made from potatoes, curry and carrots in a deep-fried pastry served with a dipping sauce. At the end of the line, one will find yogurt sauces and dessert options, including Rice Kheer, a type of sweet rice pudding. Dozens of options are available on the full-service menu, with vegetarian and vegan friendly alternatives by request.

THAI PAPAYA

Chiradaj "Joe" and Kantima "Thim" Potchanant opened Thai Papaya Cuisine in 2008 in the Melmar Plaza on Virginia Street before moving into a palatial space at 1434 Tutor Lane on Evansville's East Side that highlights their Thai heritage. Joe first came to the United States in 1975 to attend school at the Lockyear Business College in Evansville, and Thim joined him in 1988 after a long-distance courtship. Thim created many of the dishes on their menu, which can be customized according to the diner's palate, as Thim remarked in a *Courier & Press* interview, "We make each plate fresh, just for you. We add spice or sweet if you want it or we make not spicy if you don't like that. We make everything custom; we control the spices so that when you take the first bite, you taste all of the flavors." There are many curry variations on the menu, as well as Pad Thai, including a savory Asian green pumpkin curry that can be served with meat or tofu. Gluten-

Thai Papaya. *Author photo.*

free alternatives, vegan and vegetarian options are available as well. In a 2009 interview, *Evansville Living* highlighted the coconut soup offering. With a coconut milk base, the soup includes is built with "lemongrass, lime leaves, mushrooms, red bell peppers, lime juice, and galanga, a Thai herb related to ginger. Used for culinary and medicinal purposes in many Asian countries, galanga is an ancient remedy touted to aid digestion. Joe also points out the health benefits of lemongrass, which fights colds and the flu (and clears your sinuses to boot)."

VIETNAMESE CUISINE

Located at 4602 Vogel Road near the Eastland Mall, Vietnamese Cuisine has been in Evansville for about ten years and specializes in pho noodle soups, hot pot dishes, bánh mì sandwiches and rice dishes like lemongrass pork, as well as other traditional Vietnamese recipes. The friendly and gregarious staff quickly get to know what customers prefer, and the service is efficient and attentive. Colorful murals adorn the walls of river delta scenes in

Vietnam, with one side showing water buffalo and the other wall highlighting a beautiful temple with women in a traditional dress, the áo dài. Vietnamese dishes are known for their use of fresh aromatic ingredients, minimal use of oils and dairy. The dishes at Vietnamese Cuisine are commonly flavored with lemongrass, ginger, mint, bird's eye chili, lime and Thai basil. Also along the walls are two framed posters highlighting the popularity and history of pho, which originated as a dish in the mid-1880s when Chinese and French cuisine influenced Vietnamese cuisine in North Vietnam. While pho soup is the most popular, coming in heaping portions, most folks order the small, which is still a giant bowl of rice noodles in a broth with cuts of beef, seafood or chicken with a side platter of green chilies, lime, fresh basil, saw herb and beansprouts for customizing the dish—there are hot chilies in pots, hoisin sauce and sriracha on each table to make the dish as spicy as the customer would like. Another popular dish is the grilled pork with noodles, Bún Thịt Nướng, a dish served on top of noodles with a salad tossed in sweet and sour dressing, served with a crispy egg roll on the side. Appetizers include spring rolls (goi cuon), egg rolls (cha gio) and wrapped pork or chicken in grape leaves. Diners should save space for a Vietnamese coffee, cà phê đá, as a dessert, a stout brew served cold with sweetened condensed milk. All dishes are available for takeout as well.

WALTON'S INTERNATIONAL COMFORT FOOD

In the historic Haynie's Corner at 956 Parrett Street in a 1909 building is a fusion restaurant named Walton's International Comfort Food. The space was originally home to the Walton Motor Company, a Packard automobile dealership and service center, then several different neighborhood grocery stores, including the Red & White Market and the Parrett Street Market. Like many other restaurants and bars in Evansville, the space owned by Chef Tim Mills is filled with repurposed and reclaimed wood, fixtures and doors from older establishments and demolished spaces. The floors of the bar area, for example, are reclaimed barn wood, and the bar panels in front of the kitchen and main bar came from the doors of the former Lopp & Lopp Law Firm in downtown Evansville. A true fusion restaurant, the eclectic menu has featured Asian, Italian, southern and midwestern favorites. Mills brought several decades of experience as a chef in Washington, D.C, New York and Evansville to Walton's in an effort to bring a menu that would

Walton's International Comfort Food. *Author photo.*

highlight innovative dishes and comfort food. Delectable side dishes include french fries with jalapeño aioli, roasted cauliflower, bleu cheese grits, turnip greens and kimchi. Main dishes include brick oven pizzas like the Pig & Fig, which is thinly sliced prosciutto with a fig jam base and gorgonzola cheese crumbles. Other dishes include German schnitzel, stuffed rainbow trout, mac 'n' cheese shepherd's pie and Korean buffalo shrimp noodles. On the smokehouse side of the menu are burnt ends as well as a take on smoked Alabama chicken. There are also shareable plates, rice bowls, salads and sandwiches. Walton's is a family-friendly establishment with large tables perfect for congregating for a celebration or a Sunday brunch. Upstairs is Fidel's, a cigar lounge that features extensive offerings of bourbon.

WOLF'S BAR-B-Q

"Where Smokey is a Good Thing!" Wolf's Bar-B-Q on Evansville's North Side at 6600 North First Avenue has been in business since Nicholas C. Wolf opened as a wholesale meat distributor that specialized in barbecue in 1927. A fire destroyed the facility in 1946, but his sons, Nicholas Wolf II and Charles Wolf, rebuilt and began Wolf's Bar-B-Q restaurant. Charles died unexpectedly in a boating accident, and Nicholas took over as sole proprietor, expanding the restaurant, and his children, Terry and Kim Wolf, have continued the legacy of the family barbecue. For almost a century, their signature tomato-based sauce has been a customer favorite on pork ribs, slow-cooked to perfection. Local lore tells stories that Tom Hanks enjoyed coming to Wolf's while on location in Evansville to film *A League of Their Own*, which used another Evansville legend, Bosse Field, that dates back to 1915 and is the third-oldest regularly used baseball stadium in the country. Wolf's is known for its barbecue buffet, and generations of Evansville families have made the trip to share a meal together. Save room for a house-made slice of decadent coconut crème, lemon meringue, chocolate cream, southern pecan or apple pie.

5

Contemporary Icons, Fine Dining and Supper Clubs

While Evansville diners enjoy their simpler dinner fares, there is also a market for gourmet treats in refined settings with menus stocked with culinary masterpieces for the more discerning dining patron. In a September 1994 interview, Kirby's chef Horst Galow offered his take on the city: "Evansville in an international city without people realizing it." To that end, one can certainly say that Evansville also has some very cosmopolitan leanings, and the restaurant scene in the revitalized neighborhoods and cultural districts attests to that. With tasting menus and paired drink suggestions, the Evansville restaurant scene is on par with much larger cities and ever growing and expanding. For the less epicurious and adventurous, there are still many traditional favorites on the menus at these contemporary icons, time-tested recipes that generations of diners have enjoyed.

ARAZU ON MAIN

Arazu has two locations in the Tristate, the original Café Arazu in Newburgh near the Ohio River and the more recent second location, Arazu on Main Street in downtown Evansville. Owner Penny Nejad has outfitted both locations with colorful décor collected from her world travels with a belief that "through food, we discover that we are more alike than we are different.

Arazu on Main. *Author photo.*

A good meal holds the unique power to unify different culture, faiths, and ethnicities. After all, sharing food is one of the world's oldest traditions." The original location opened in 2010 in a former 1800s icehouse. Nejad's menus reflects Persian, Indian and Mediterranean dishes that are presented as rich plates of savory comfort foods like tandoori butter chicken refined to a level comfortable for the midwestern palate. The 415 Main Street location in Evansville opened in 2015 in the building that used to house the Jungle coffeehouse. Unique menu items include the appetizer called Cuban Cigars, an eggroll filled with Cuban-style fried beef, and the Polynesian pork sandwich, consisting of pork tenderloin sautéed with sweet red onions, banana peppers and pineapple on a kaiser roll with mixed greens and teriyaki sauce dressing.

BRU BURGER (EVANSVILLE GREYHOUND STATION)

The renaissance story of Evansville's downtown in the last several years would not be complete without a rendition of the transformation of the iconic Greyhound Station now home to Indianapolis-based chain Bru Burger since 2016. Indiana Landmarks undertook the extension restoration of the station and carefully preserved memorabilia unearthed during construction—now part of the interior décor. Photos, receipts, a wallet, ledger books and even a discarded sketchbook were found. Built in the late 1930s, the Art Moderne station was designed by Louisville, Kentucky–based architect William Arrasmith and operated as a bus terminal until the 1990s. According to Marsh Davis of Indiana Landmarks, "It's one of the most distinctive buildings in the state. It's all shiny, enameled metal panels on the outside. And to add to that, it has some really wonderful neon, with the running dog motif that's used by Greyhound....That in itself makes this building an eye-catching landmark." Rumor has it that the City of Evansville originally intended to demolish the building and build a gas station in its place, but Indiana Landmarks stepped in, taking ownership in 2013 with the intention to renovate and find a tenant for adaptive reuse. It was a $2.3 million rehabilitation project that included removing the exterior metal panels and resurfacing them, restoring the neon and completely gutting the interior except for architectural features like the tile floors and metal railings of the staircase to the second floor.

This page: Old Greyhound Station (Bru Burger). *Courtesy of Evansville Vanderburgh Public Library, Evansville Postcard Collection.*

Right: Bru Burger. *Author photo*.

Below: Bru Burger side bus terminal, now open-air seating. *Author photo*.

Bru Burger has a delightful menu of made-from-scratch gourmet burgers, salads and appetizers as well as an extensive selection of craft beers and cocktails. From barbecue nachos to sriracha Caesar salads and lamb burgers with sides of onion rings, the taste profile is eclectic. The burgers include a wide variety of bases like beef, turkey, lamb, a vegetarian garbanzo bean and mushroom, vegan quinoa, grilled portabella, grilled mahi-mahi and a battered cod option. More recently, the restaurant has incorporated the vegan friendly Impossible burger and tries to source produce from Indiana farmers like Fischer Farms locally and Gunthorp Farms from northern Indiana, delivered by Piazza Produce. All sauces are made in-house. Always busy, the location has dining along the main floor, upstairs and in a covered patio perfect for dining alfresco.

COMFORT / CROSS-EYED CRICKET

To say that down-home cooking is beloved by the Tristate would be a bit of an understatement, and very few establishments provide a better greasy spoon experience than the original Cross-Eyed Cricket. Recently, however, Josh Tudela, whose family owns the original, has elevated that experience with Comfort by Cross-Eyed Cricket in a historic 1857 building at the corner of Main and Third Streets in downtown Evansville. The original Cross-Eyed Cricket is on Pennsylvania Street on the West Side off the Lloyd Expressway. Fernando Tudela, who has a wide range of restaurant experience from Weinbach Cafeteria to Evans Café, made the Cross-Eyed Cricket into a beloved success story. The 1988 opening was reviewed by the *Courier & Press*, which called it "honest food at honest prices" and raved about the house-made vegetable soup and the affordably priced plate lunches. Indeed, the reviewers, Sara Anne Corrigan and Keith Rice, said the lunch of a dressed hamburger with a side of onion rings was so generously portioned that they were so full that "supper was out of the question later in the day."

Comfort is housed in the former home of the Farmer's Daughter (see chapter 1) at 230 Main Street, and the Tudelas spent two years renovating and reconstructing the space into a bespoke and charming farm-to-table inspired restaurant. On the menu are favorites from the original location like meatloaf, chicken and dumplings, fried chicken and salmon. Each table receives a basket of biscuits with a side of strawberry-infused butter.

Comfort by Cross Eyed Cricket. *Author photo.*

But the menu is not just familiar favorites. Tudela brought in Le Cordon Bleu College of Culinary Arts–trained chef Donielle Taylor and chef Diego Melendrez, who has experience in fine dining from California, as well as Andy Wood, a beverage director, to infuse the menu with unique culinary offerings that set Comfort apart from its predecessor and on path with the latest gastronomic trends. In a recent *Evansville Living* restaurant feature, Wood opined, "Some of the flavors are a little esoteric or a little different, but I think that's something Evansville is ready for. To have the classics but to come in and be able to taste a drink that's smoky or a drink that's bitter or a drink that's herbaceous—introducing new stuff to people. I'm always impressed by Evansville at how willing they are to experiment." Most recently, the folks behind Comfort teamed up with Proper Coffee and have added a new element next door, Parlor Doughnuts, which specializes in custom-made gourmet doughnuts, including gluten-free and vegan options.

CORK 'N CLEAVER

Part of a national chain of restaurants, Evansville's Cork 'N Cleaver, at 650 South Hebron Avenue, opened in 1974. The very first Cork 'N Cleaver opened in Scottsdale, Arizona, in 1964. Of the original eighty locations, only three remain in business: Evansville; Fort Wayne, Indiana; and, Fargo, North Dakota. The chain of steakhouses features casual southwestern décor and a menu that centers on aged hand-cut steaks, prime rib, fish, seafood and pasta dishes. On the side, diners can enjoy a lavish salad bar with heaps of fresh vegetables, fruits and house-made dressing. Owner since 2001, a restaurant veteran of the Ashley Grill, La Strada and Outback Steakhouse, Steve Bennett maintains the Evansville location and attributes the Cork's success to longtime customers and the community, which continue to make the restaurant a special dinner spot. In a recent *Courier & Press* restaurant review, Bennett remarked, "We have such great support from the community, that's the thing. I see kids coming in with their parents, and then 15 years later I'm seeing them come in with their own kids. We have sons and fathers coming in to buy each other gift certificates for Christmas. We see the same faces. I'll see a regular guest has a reservation, so I'll save their favorite booth, or make sure we have the Merlot they like. The guests are part of our family." The menu has not changed significantly in the last several decades, nor has the building. In an article in *Evansville Living*, Bennett opined, "We've been blessed and have stayed busy." Part of the success can be attributed to the old-school steakhouse charm, a place with exquisite and quality dishes that are always consistent. Indeed, Bennett tells of a story when the parent company tried to change the Cork restaurants to a different theme called the Lost Dutchman in the 1990s before he bought the Evansville location, "They added rotisserie chicken, ribs and huge monster stuffed baked potatoes…. They painted the beams this awful bright teal blue. The regulars did not like it one bit." According to Bennett, the proprietors changed the menus back within a month, but "the teal color stayed for a long time. When we bought it, within six months we painted the beams brown like they are now. It softened it a bit from the black iron deal it was in the beginning." "It's a great level of support we've had all these years," owner Steve Bennett said. "Evansville embraced us as a hometown restaurant even when the Cork N' Cleaver was still a chain. We keep it simple, work on quality, prep to run out and own up to our mistakes. We make them like anyone else, and we try to handle those the way we want to be treated. We've been very fortunate, and the community has been good to us, and we try to support local business." The Cork is open for lunch and dinner throughout the week, serving dinner only on weekends, and offers an early bird menu between 4:00 p.m. and 5:30 p.m. daily.

EVANSVILLE COUNTRY CLUB

The Evansville Country Club on the North Side of town at 3810 Stringtown Road has a history that dates back to 1900 when prominent families would take the Evansville-Vincennes cable car to a private lake near Pigeon Creek for hunting and fishing excursions. The original club had 101 members, and eventually the club reorganized in 1908 to focus on the sport of golf. By 1927, the club had an eighteen-hole course that has remained a popular private course in the Evansville region in the verdant hills of the North Side. Now a nearly seven-hundred-member family operation, the Evansville Country Club offers not only golf but also dining, swimming and social activities. A private club, the social membership includes dining with an executive chef on staff and a wide ranging of tastes.

Evansville Country Club. *Courtesy of the University of Southern Indiana.*

HAUB'S STEAK HOUSE

Farther north of Evansville but a popular Tristate location is the Haub's Steak House in Haubstdt up in Gibson County. Its building has a history that began in 1900 as a grain warehouse, but the steakhouse opened in 1970 under the leadership of the Haley family, who fairly recently turned over operations to the Ungetheim family. The Ungetheims have had quite a bit of experience in local favorites with the Hornet's Nest (see chapter 2). All of the meat has been aged and hand cut, frequently earning the location the honor of best of awards from *Courier & Press* and in *Evansville Living* over the years. The menu features many cuts of beef as well as seafood, duck, pork, chicken options and barbecue. House features include tournedos of beef presented with bordelaise sauce topped with mushrooms; Coquille St. Jacques, made of fresh scallops broiled with mushrooms in a wine cream sauce; and Seafood Au Gratin, made with a blend of shrimp, snow crab and haddock chunks in tangy cheese sauce, then broiled. A favorite of Kathy Oeth's, her go-to meal is a medium-well steak accompanied by cauliflower salad with bread pudding for dessert. The cauliflower salad is florets tossed with house dressing, lettuce and bacon. Dessert options include ice cream drinks with brandy, Chambord, Kahlua or amaretto as well as multiple cheesecakes, mud pie and pecan pie.

Haub's Steak House. *Author photo.*

HOUSE OF COMO

On old Highway 41, now South Kentucky Avenue, is one of the most unique restaurants in all of the Tristate, the House of Como. House of Como has the distinction of being one of the last restaurants to persevere along old Highway 41, South Kentucky Avenue. In the 1950s and 1960s, this area was home to a number of restaurants, including Evans Cafe, Farmer's Daughter and the Humpty Dumpty. Today, the Roca Bar and House of Como continue the tradition as the neighborhoods change over time. Opened by George Hage in 1960, the kitschy staple outfitted with year-round Christmas decorations has a menu filled with decadent Greek and Mediterranean dishes as well as steaks with recipes inspired by Hage's Lebanese background. The original location was once the Brown Derby, which opened in 1932 and was a popular gambling, dancing and dining night spot connected to twenty-one guest cottages. The current location at 2700 South Kentucky opened in 1969 after a fire damaged the original location. Although a May 2011 fire forced the current restaurant to close for a little over a year, the House of Como reopened in November 2012 and continues to be a cash-only destination spot for locals and tourists alike. Some of the dishes most loved by patrons are the djage, or baked chicken with white rice and pine nut dressing; kibi seneya, baked finely ground

House of Como. *Author photo.*

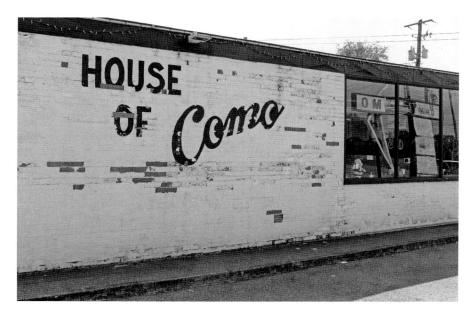

House of Como. *Author photo.*

meat with wheat; and yebra malfoof, rolled cabbage leaves with meat. After George passed away, his wife, Martha, continued to operate the restaurant with their daughters Laura and Libby. One can see patrons who have driven from Chicago or St. Louis to get their fix of Middle Eastern, Italian and American dishes, with the favorites being Lebanese shish kebab, eggplant casserole and lamb chops.

LOG INN

While many taverns have their start as historic stage coach stops, the Log Inn, built about 1825, was along the trail between Evansville, Vincennes and Terre Haute and claims that in 1844, Abraham Lincoln stopped here while stumping for presidential candidate Henry Clay, the famed Kentucky politician known as the Great Compromiser. The original log structure can be seen in the interior of the now vastly expanded and remodeled space. Recognized as the oldest continuously operating restaurant in the state of Indiana, the Log Inn sits twelve miles north of Evansville's downtown off North Highway 41 at 12653 S. 200 E in Warrenton. Named after Revolutionary War hero

Log Inn. *Author photo.*

General Joseph Warren, the little hamlet included early owner of the Log Inn Henry Haub, who founded the town of Haubstadt in 1855. Meier Heiman, a German Jewish settler, took over the stop in 1852 and expanded the building to include a grocery and dry goods shop, tavern and dance hall. It was a popular destination for construction workers on the Wabash Canal. Joe Reinhart took over ownership and operations in 1895 and then sold it later to the George Memmer family. Both owners focused on reinforcing the building and renovating, obfuscating the humble original log edifice. The current operation began in 1947 with Pete Rettig and his wife. Victoria, who renovated the building in 1965 to show its history, including exposing the log walls in the interior and renaming it the Log Inn. Their daughter, Rita, and her husband, Gene Elpers, took over in 1978, and it is now run by Daryl Elpers, Trish Elpers, their sister Kathy Holzmeyer and their families. Their menu consists of family-style dinners featuring fried chicken, which has won many *Courier & Press* and *Evansville Living* awards. The recipe for the chicken comes from a family recipe that they have prepared in-house since the 1960s with chickens sourced from local farmers via Farm Boy. In a recent news interview, Kathy Holzmeyer shared, "We can't tell you everything. But we can tell you that the flour comes from Nunn-Better, which is local, and we use salt and pepper and we have a special spice mixture that we mix in the

Log Inn. *Author photo.*

flour." The restaurant preps about 675 whole chickens a week. The menu is stocked with local and fresh ingredients, such as Dewig's country ham and house-roasted roast beef, with side of house-cut German fries or hand-mashed potatoes. Families have their choice of homestyle meals served to their table on platters. Each diner gets to choose half a chicken, ham or roast beef and plenty of mashed potatoes, gravy, vegetables, slaw and hot rolls will be placed on the table as accompaniments. For those after a less family-style option, there are lots of à la carte plates, including cheeseburgers and catfish filets, as well as seafood platters. Desserts are pretty legendary, including the Fluffy Peanut Butter Pie.

Log Inn's Fluffy Peanut Butter Pie

1 (8-ounce) package cream cheese, softened
¾ cup peanut butter, smooth or crunchy
1 cup powdered sugar
½ cup milk
9 ounces whipped cream topping
9-inch graham cracker crust
½ cup finely chopped peanuts (optional)

Beat cheese until soft and fluffy. Add peanut butter and sugar gradually and beat. Slowly add milk into the mixture. Fold in whipped topping and pour into prepared crust. Sprinkle on nuts and freeze. Remove from freezer about 15 minutes before serving. Makes 1 pie.

—https://janceys.blogspot.com/2012/11/log-inns-fluffy-peanut-butter-pie.html

MADELEINE'S

Madeleine's. *Author photo.*

Madeleine's creates dishes that are elegant works of art in its show kitchen, complemented by an extensive wine cellar, decadent pastries and an intimate classic fine-dining room. Madeleine's, at 423 Southeast Second Street near Haynie's Corner and the Historic District, has the distinction of being the first fusion restaurant in the area. A creative and spontaneous menu highlights eclectic specialty dishes that range from Italian, Asian, French and Spanish influences. The regular menu offers rack of lamb with a mustard barbecue sauce, aged blackened bone-in ribeye, Philadelphia strip steak and coffee-encrusted filet mignon. Dishes are paired with seasonal produce and a fine selection of wine and liquor nestled into a boutique setting in the historic district. *Evansville Living* magazine described it thus: "Think of it as Pacific Rim meeting Spanish and Classic American regional cuisines with the occasional European touch." Madeleine's is a sister business to Walton's International Comfort Foods.

SAUCED

Part of the Haynie's Corner Art District's renaissance since 2014, Sauced is housed in a late nineteenth-century Victorian home at 1113 Parrett Strett under the leadership of Scott Schymik, who also owns Kirby's Private Dining, a catering service and venue. Kirby's is named after Kirby's Old Kentucky Barbecue (see chapter 1), one more venue that has passed on but whose influence remains in the Evansville restaurant scene. Sauced is an intimate atmosphere with just eighty-five seats in three rooms displaying local artwork and vintage items in the renovated space of the former home. Schymik highlights his family history in the restaurant business with family portraits and a vintage menu from his grandparents' restaurant, the Peacock. From his family, Schymik has sourced a signature spaghetti with meat sauce and fried chicken inspired by his grandparents' menu. Sauced focuses on dishes made from vegetables grown in its own gardens and locally sourced produce and meats. A customer favorite is the Ratano Carpaccio, a lightly seared tenderloin paired with parsley, horseradish, marinated mushrooms and pickled red onions. The decorations include a sign for an Evansville lost legend, the Blue Bar nightclub, which used to be in the old Lincoln Hotel off Main and Fifth Street. It was a watering hole in the 1950s and 1960s that saw blues musicians on the rise, including saxophonist Boots Randolph, who wrote the song, "Yakkity Sax."

Sauced. *Author photo.*

WESTERN RIBEYE

The Nix family has owned Western Ribeye & Ribs at 1401 North Boeke Road since 1975 when Harold Nix opened the restaurant with just three menu items: ribeye, filet and lobster. Current owners David and Dan Nix have carried on the family tradition since 1985. Known for fine cuts of steak, barbecue ribs, fried chicken, surf and turf and an extensive salad bar, the restaurant also has banquet and private meeting rooms. Their salad bar is the second in Evansville's history, after the now closed Andy's and Steak and Barrel featured the first. Their soups are all house-made, including the popular chili, French onion and steak soup with fresh vegetables in a brown broth. All of the vegetables on the salad bar are house cut to make sure they are served at the peak of their freshness. You can also find pickled herring on the salad bar, a unique rarity in this region. In September 2019, David Nix spoke to the *Evansville Courier & Press* about the restaurant's success: "We stick to what we know best, which is consistent product and service.... You know what to expect when you get in here. The salad bar is always fresh and healthy, we use high-quality products, and the menu has a good variety—steak, salmon, some chicken and also the ribs and pork chops. Another thing is that we can accommodate tables of 10–20 people and every weekend we have many large groups. Space is expensive today, and newer restaurants keep space tight and need to turn tables faster, but when you have a birthday party or anniversary, they want to socialize without feeling rushed."

Afterthought

Decades after the closing of Kirby's Old Kentucky Barbecue, Kirby's son, Jim Williams, was still reminiscing about how food can bring a community together, and after a successful and eclectic career as the founder of Holiday Travel Service, Jim had a new project on his horizon, Kirby's Fine Dining in Haynie's Corner. Kirby's opened on April 17, 1990, in two Victorian-era houses with a grand ballroom built to connect the two buildings in 1992. Able to host 350 guests for private parties and events, Kirby's was at the forefront of the renaissance of Haynie's Corner, as one September 1994 *Courier & Press* article noted, "in a big old house once condemned and in a part of town where other businesses had tried and failed." From his international travel experiences, Jim brought on board a world-renowned master chef, Horst Galow, who provided a Westphalian Mushroom Tart recipe for the *Courier* piece. Galow and Williams met in 1977 in the Dominican Republic. Galow grew up in Dortmund, Germany, and worked in the restaurant industry in Belgium, Switzerland, Spain, England, France, the Canary Islands, Argentina, Malta and the Dominican Republic. Jim was a serial entrepreneur, according to his daughter Julie, and spent five years with Kirby's before moving on to new adventures. Kirby's Private Dining has been owned since 2006 by Scott Schymik, who trained under Galow at Kirby's and is another restaurateur (creator of Sauced and Schymik's Kitchen) and vibrant leader in Haynie's Corner. Horst Galow's recipes are still a part of Kirby's catering menu.

Westphalian Mushroom Tart

3 hamburger buns without sesame seeds
½ pound ground pork
½ pound ground beef
¼ cup butter
1 bunch green onions
1 ½ pounds mixed brown mushrooms
Salt and coarse pepper for seasoning
1 teaspoon fresh thyme leaves
1 clove garlic
1 teaspoon marjoram leaves
2 ounces dry white wine or dry sherry
3 large eggs
1 cup whipping cream
Paprika (optional)

Soak buns in water. In large mixing bowl, combine ground meat and let rest at room temperature. In a skillet, melt three-fourths of the butter. Chop the green onions. Wash the mushrooms and cut in quarters. Add onions and mushrooms to butter; sauté until glazing appears. Season with salt and pepper; add herbs and white wine. Boil up thoroughly; set aside to cool. Squeeze bread as dry as possible; add to meat. Season meat with salt and pepper to taste. Add half of the eggs and half of the cream to meat. Blend in the cooled mushroom sauté; mix thoroughly by hand. Use rest of butter to line spring-form pan. Fill mixture firmly into spring form. Whip up remaining egg and cream; add paprika, salt and pepper. Pour over tart. Bake at 350 degrees for 50 to 55 minutes. Serve with a tomato sauce if desired and a green vegetable such as broccoli, brussels sprouts or asparagus spears.

—*Evansville Courier & Press*, September 21, 1994, "Take a Big Old House in An Unlikely Neighborhood, Add a Master Chef and a Travel Pro, and, Voila, You Get…Cultured Cuisine"

Evansville restaurant history is in the throes of a renaissance as new establishments mingle with cherished eateries in historic neighborhoods and cultural districts. With the new Indiana University partnership medical center downtown and the Ford Center stadium, attention to revitalizing downtown is at an all-time high. Cultural events, food trucks and festivals are all a part of the Evansville scene. Some are as small and local as Porchfests in neighborhoods. Local breweries have flourished in the past few years as Evansville reclaims its brewing traditions all over the city. Independent restaurants are a big component to the renaissance of Evansville eateries. Take the time to check out spots downtown, in Jacobsville and on North Main Street, Haynie's Corner, along Franklin Street on the near West Side, near the University of Evansville, farther east out to Newburgh and out along the old roads to the little taverns that have stood the test of time. Whether you're looking for an adventurous culinary night out or to tuck into a favorite time-tested comfort food, be sure to go out and support Evansville's eclectic eateries.

Haynie's Corner Market. *Author photo.*

Bibliography

Evansville Courier & Press.

Evansville Courier.

Evansville Living.

Evansville Press.

Greater Evansville, Southwest Indiana. https://eisforeveryone.com.

Historic Evansville. http://historicevansville.com.

Reid Duffy's Guide to Indiana's Favorite Restaurants. Indianapolis: Indiana University Press, 2006.

River Cities Oral History Project.

Russell, Joan. "The History of the American Diner." *Paste*, October 18, 2016. pastemagazine.com.

Vanderburgh County Historical Society. "Discover Indiana: A Sense of Community: Historic Taverns of Vanderburgh County." 2019.

Vanderburgh County Historical Society. http://www.vchshistory.org.

Willard Library. Evansville Historic Photo Collection. https://willard.lib.in.us/research/archives/historic-photo-collection.

About the Author

K ristalyn Shefveland is a University of Southern Indiana professor in the Department of History and has lived in Evansville since 2010. A native of Wabasha, Minnesota, and North Ridgeville, Ohio, she grew up hearing stories of giant catfish in the upper Mississippi River and eating Frank's Bratwursts with kraut on a soft roll topped with stadium mustard in the gallery of the Cleveland Westside Market. A scholar of the American South and the Native Southeast, Shefveland enjoys the ways in which history and foodways can intersect and is the creator of the *River Cities Oral History Project*, a collaborative effort at the University of Southern Indiana that seeks to collect memories and stories about the Tristate region. She is the author of *Anglo-Native Virginia: Trade, Conversion, and Indian Slavery in the Old Dominion, 1646–1722* (University of Georgia Press, 2016).